DARK AGE BRITAIN

SO FEW LIVES

So few lives divide us; a hundred years
  Carry three lives, and when the party's over,
The century drained dry, it yet appears
  For patient spade suddenly to uncover,
Frail, and a little chipped, the perfume gone
  Of the dead wine. But in the bottle yet
We see the vanished ruby that glowed and shone
  During those faded years when the wine was set
In those three glasses. Thirty men at most
  Fill out a thousand years, each with his glass,
Laughing at table, no unbodied ghost
  But a friend speaking, though the hours pass
    So swiftly from the bottle to the tomb;
    Their faces shine within my shadowed room.

HENRY MARSH

Beram Saklatvala

DARK AGE BRITAIN

Some Sources of History

ARCHON BOOKS 1970

ISBN 0-208-01153-6

This edition published in the United States of America 1970
by Archon Books, Hamden, Connecticut

Printed in Great Britain

CONTENTS

LIST OF ILLUSTRATIONS

PLATES

MAPS

PROLOGUE

THE frontier that divides prehistory from history is not precise and its position on the map of time varies from land to land. Prehistory—the period for which there are no written records—continued in Britain long after the peoples around the Mediterranean had mastered the art of writing and had used it to celebrate the achievements of their ancestors and to record the forms and values of their own societies.

The dawn is never abrupt. Long before sunrise, when the earth is still hidden in impenetrable darkness, the sky in the east grows grey and the shapes of clouds can be indistinctly perceived. Features of the landscape emerge slowly, still without colour and still imprecise of form. Slowly the mystery of the night gives way to day's beauty as colours and details leap forward from the darkness into the bright sunlight.

So it was with Britain. Centuries before the Christian era, Mediterranean writers had referred to her. But Britain's true recorded history begins in AD 43 when Aulus Plautius, a Roman senator acting on the orders of the Emperor Claudius, led four legions of troops from Gaul to conquer the island. Julius Caesar had fruitlessly come twice on the same adventure nearly 100 years before and had written an account of his campaigns. But the island was still virtually unknown to the Roman world and at first the troops of Aulus Plautius (according to Cassius Dio) refused to obey orders to embark and fight a battle beyond the frontiers of the known world. Once they had sailed, however, their transports cruising up-channel, and they themselves making an unopposed landing on the coast of Kent, the dawn of history finally broke over the island. From that time onwards Britain's destiny was linked with that of Rome, and there were many writers to chronicle events in the province. For nearly 400 years evidence is plentiful and witnesses abundant.

Caesar's own report of his two campaigns in Britain are contained in Books IV and V of his famous work De Bello Gallico, *The War in Gaul.* He records that before his first expedition he sent one ship, under the command of Gaius Volusenus, to reconnoitre the coast and to find a suitable landing place, 'for the Gauls knew nothing about this'. He also questioned traders, hoping to obtain from them details of the inhabitants of Britain, their military strength and tactics, and to learn something of the harbours. News of his intentions reached the Britons, and they sent a deputation promising peace. He reassured them and sent them home accompanied by Commius, whom he had appointed king over one of the tribes in Gaul. All this suggests that there was a good deal of intercourse between Gaul and Britain, and that the Gauls knew much more about the island than they were prepared to disclose to Caesar.

After five days Volusenus returned with such intelligence as he had been able to gather, not having landed but merely sailing along the coast. The Roman army, consisting of two legions (about 10,000 men), boarded the transports and the fleet of eighty ships set sail. Eighteen further vessels, carrying the cavalry, were gathered eight miles away. These were unable to sail because of contrary winds, with the result that Caesar was to find himself woefully short of horsemen.

They made landfall by steep cliffs which so dominated the beach 'that it was possible to throw a missile from the high ground on to the shore': this is generally taken to be a description of Dover. Caesar's ships accordingly stood off, awaited a favourable wind, and sailed seven miles down the coast where, on a shelving beach, the crews ran the transports aground.

The Britons rode their horses into the sea to meet the Roman troops as they leapt from the ships and there was a moment of near panic, with the unnerved soldiers unwilling to face the unfamiliar dangers. The day was saved by the courage of the standard-bearer of the Tenth Legion, who jumped into the water and, carrying the standard aloft, advanced against the enemy. The Britons were beaten and sent Caesar's envoy, Commius, to sue for peace on their behalf. Caesar sternly rebuked them. Why, after sending a peaceful deputation to him in Gaul, had they opposed his landing? His attitude must have struck the Britons as unreasonable and they in turn might well have asked why—when they had promised peace—he had landed in their island with 10,000 men! Caesar took hostages from the Britons and an uneasy truce was arranged.

Three days later there was a full moon and a high tide which waterlogged the beached ships, damaged most of those anchored off-shore and utterly destroyed several. The Britons, knowing Caesar's lack of cavalry and seeing the damage to his fleet, broke the truce and resumed hostilities. Caesar cannibalised his wrecked galleys, using the timbers and metal fittings of the worst damaged to repair the others, and so limited his total losses to twelve ships. The Seventh Legion was ambushed while out foraging for corn and Caesar's words—'a few were killed'—suggest that there were fairly heavy casualties. After a further sharp engagement, Caesar demanded more hostages and was content to re-embark his troops, returning to Gaul with very little accomplished and with the loss of many ships and not a few men.

In the following year he came again to Britain. The size of the forces he assembled is a measure of the respect he now had for the Britons' prowess. He describes their skill with their war chariots: they could drive at full gallop down steep slopes; they could check and turn in a moment; the charioteers could run along the harness-pole, stand on the yoke, and nimbly step backwards into the chariot.

So now he embarked not two legions but five, and no fewer than 2,000 cavalry. This formidable army, in a massive fleet of 800 ships, made an unopposed landing about midday, having been at sea since dusk on the previous evening. (Such a large fleet was not to cross the channel again until D-Day in 1944.) Having garrisoned his beach-head camp, Caesar struck inland, making a night march of some twelve miles. In the battle which followed, the Seventh Legion (perhaps grimly remembering the ambush of the year before) vigorously attacked and cleared the Britons from their defensive position.

Caesar tells us that the Britons were led by Cassivellaunus (whom we shall meet again in legend and fable). His territory was bounded to the south by a river called the Thames (*Tamesis*) about eighty miles from the sea. There follows an excellent and full description of the land and its inhabitants. According to tradition (he wrote), the Britons were aboriginal. But the maritime districts were inhabited by descendants of continental invaders. The population was dense and farms, similar to those in Gaul, were numerous and well stocked with cattle. (We must remember that Caesar was describing only the extreme south-east of Britain.) Although there were some gold coins the chief currency was iron bars of a fixed weight. Tin was mined but bronze had to be imported.

He described the island as triangular, with the southern side 500 miles long, 'bending westwards towards Spain'. The error of placing the western coast of Britain opposite and close to Spain was repeated by later writers and is possibly the origin of the tales we shall consider later of people from Spain sailing to Britain and settling there after strange and magical adventures.

Caesar noted the existence of Ireland and of the Isle of 'Mona'—possibly the Isle of Man. He also noted that the nights (measured with a water-clock) were longer than in Gaul.

He wrote of Kent as being the most civilised region, and described its culture as similar to that of Gaul. He added a few interesting details: that the Britons stained themselves blue with woad, that they grew moustaches and shaved their bodies. Group marriage was an accepted institution (presumably among some of the pre-Celtic people), with ten or twelve men having wives in common.

Caesar also wrote of the Trinovantes, the strongest tribe in the south-east, whose king had earlier been slain by Cassivellaunus. The dead king's son had gone to Gaul to join Caesar. The Trinovantes are later seen again, disguised by myth as the New Trojans, whose ancestors were said to have sailed to Britain after the sack of Troy! Legends can grow from the unlikeliest origins, even from the dry pages of a general's memoirs.

The picture that emerges is fairly clear. Britain was a group of rival kingdoms and Caesar was able to exploit the rivalry between Cassivellaunus and the Trinovantes. Levels of culture varied from the primitive to the highly sophisticated. There were towns and farms, fairly abundant trade and an ability to offer effective resistance even to the invincible Roman army.

The next notable Roman author to deal with Britain was Tacitus, writing about 150 years after Caesar's expeditions. By his day some fifty years had passed since the occupation of the south-east of the island by the legions of Claudius. Roman rule was stabilised and the province fully organised. Rome's motives for the occupation were partly political—Caesar had noted that Britain was a refuge for dissident elements in Gaul—and partly economic. Strabo had listed Britain's useful exports as wheat, cattle, slaves, hunting dogs, gold and silver.

Tacitus had married the daughter of Agricola, a very distinguished Roman of Gallic descent. Agricola was made consul in AD 77 and later that year was appointed governor of Britain. He held this office for seven years during which time he completed the conquest of what is now Wales and fought successfully in the hills of Caledonia. He was recalled by the Emperor Domitian—prematurely, in his friends' view. Tacitus, a devoted admirer of his father-in-law, wrote a biography of him (the *Agricola*), probably in AD 97 or 98; much of the book consists of a defence and vindication of Agricola and an attack on those who recalled him from Britain with his task of pacification and reorganisation still incomplete.

Of greater interest in the present context is Tacitus's description of Britain, in his chapters 10-12. It was the largest of all the islands brought under Roman rule. 'In the east' he wrote, 'it faces Germany, in the west it extends towards Spain, and in the south it is visible from Gaul. In the north it lies opposite no other lands, but its shores are pounded by a vast and open sea.' He quoted an earlier writer who had likened Britain to a double-headed axe; but he added that this was true only if Caledonia were omitted, since a huge wedge-shaped piece of land jutted out beyond. A Roman fleet had sailed round Britain, thereby proving it to be an island. Islands hitherto unknown, called the *Orcades* (Orkneys) had been discovered and conquered. He describes the stormy northern seas and then gives an account of the inhabitants.

Physical characteristics varied. The Caledonians were red-headed and heavily built, suggesting a Germanic origin. The Silures in the west, swarthy and with curly hair, probably came from Spain which lies opposite them. (The legend is growing.) Those living opposite Gaul were like the Gauls: Tacitus argued that this was not due simply to similar climates producing similar types, but to the presence of emigrants from Gaul, adducing as evidence (very logically) the similarity between the religions of the two nations. But the Britons—a people whom no long period of peace had softened—were the more ferocious. Those of the Britons who had long been conquered had degenerated. 'The rest are still what the Gauls once were.'

They were strong in infantry. Some tribes fought with chariots and the charioteers were men of high rank. Once they had been ruled by kings, but they were now divided into factions under many chiefs. 'The greatest advantage for us in dealing with these tribes is that they do not act in concert.' We shall see how this lack of unity among the Britons persisted through many centuries; the Anglo-Saxons, like the Romans, were to find that disunity among the Britons was to help them conquer the island.

Turning to the natural resources of Britain, Tacitus wrote that, apart from the olive and the vine, all other produce grew abundantly in the damp climate. Gold, silver and other metals were available. There were also pearls, but of a poor colour. The Britons bore taxes cheerfully, provided there was no oppression. 'They have been conquered but not enslaved.'

For the rest, Tacitus described Agricola's various campaigns in Britain, including his victory over the wild tribes of Caledonia.

Tacitus also included lengthy passages on Britain in his *Annals* and we can follow in detail such matters as the rising of Queen Boudicca and the achievements of various governors.

Pliny in his *Natural History*, which he dedicated to the Emperor Titus in AD 77, devoted a brief chapter to Britain and Ireland, recorded that the true name of Britain was Albion, gave its size and the distance of the crossing from Gaul, mentioned the 'wood of Caledonia', and listed the islands that lie scattered over its seas. Hadrian's biographer Aelius Spartianus tells us that one of the Emperor's friends wrote a few lines of doggerel to celebrate Hadrian's visit to the island:

> I would hate to be poor Caesar
> Walking through the lands of Britain . . .

The Romans mapped the island, constructed a network of roads and worked out routes from city to city. Then when Rome fell to the triumphant Goths in AD 410, her power vanished from Britain. The Romanised Britains, no longer protected by the armies or wisdom of Rome, fought long and courageously against the troubles which beset them and by which they were finally overwhelmed. The sun of history sets, and again the story of Britain is enveloped in darkness. Troops were brought from Germany under their leader Hengist (events to be considered later) in a vain attempt to stiffen the resistance of the local armies; they mutinied and finally seized almost all of the once-proud province; these men were the first English. Continental writers knew little of what was taking place in the lost island and recorded only rumours and fables.

But the darkness was not total. One or two Britons recorded the tragedy of their overthrow for later ages. The invaders, too, kept their records and one at least among them produced a scientific and methodical history of his people. Later when Britain became settled, and the new kingdom of England was finally established, there were men who sought to peer through 'the dark backward and abysm of time' to find out what had happened between the fall of Roman power and the building of the kingdom of England. That kingdom may be said to have been finally established by King Alfred in the ninth century. Because of the encouragement he gave to scholarship and the keeping of records, from his day the history of England is relatively well documented.

The purpose of this book is to examine the most important writers, both British and English, who can throw light upon the history of Britain from the time of the first coming of the English to the reign of Alfred. The period is long, spanning some five centuries.

The first 200 years were almost wholly taken up by the struggle between the Romanised Britons and the invading Anglo-Saxons. These are perhaps the darkest and most mysterious centuries of all British history. The witnesses are few. First in time as well as in importance is Gildas, dubbed the Wise. He lived in the sixth century, about 150 years after the end of Roman rule in Britain, and wrote a history of the tragic events which had befallen his people the Britons, mourning their overthrow by the Anglo-Saxons.

Next is Nennius, about whom little is known, but whose writings clearly embody at least some material dating from the same period as Gildas and whose words help to fill in some of the details. Two other documents are also of some assistance: the *Annales Cambriae* (the *Welsh Annals*), and *Brut y Tywysogion* (the *Chronicle of the Princes of Wales*). All four documents naturally tell the story from the point of view of the Britons.

Once the invading Anglo-Saxons had been converted to

Christianity (by St Augustine from 597 onwards) and some of them acquired a little learning, they too began to maintain records; the *Anglo-Saxon Chronicle* gives the narrative from their point of view from their first arrival to the twelfth century. The conflict between the Britons and the Anglo-Saxons became of secondary importance and during the succeeding centuries it is the story of the foundation and growth of England that takes pride of place. In addition to the *Anglo-Saxon Chronicle* there is the Venerable Bede's magnificent *Ecclesiastical History of the English People* (AD 731), a work startlingly ahead of its time in scholarship and scientific method. Bede's work dominated and influenced the writing of English history. King Alfred later translated Bede's Latin into English and, at the same time, arranged for the maintaining of the *Anglo-Saxon Chronicle* in an orderly fashion. Bishop Asser, Alfred's tutor who assisted the king in his literary labours, wrote a life of King Alfred, from which much may be learned.

After the Norman Conquest there was a revival of interest in early British history. William, a monk of Malmesbury (who died some time after 1142), and of mixed English and Norman descent, wrote a fine and thorough *History of the Kings of England.*

And the twelfth century saw the beginning of legendary history, with accuracy sacrificed to romance and truth to legend. Geoffrey of Monmouth (who died some time after 1147), a Welshman descended from the original Britons, and a man of immense energy and imagination, wrote *The History of the Britons.*

These are the witnesses to be examined in this book.

I

GILDAS THE WISE

BY the middle of the fifth century there had been nearly fifty years of strife and desolation since the last of the Roman armies had sailed from Britain. It was only the very old who could remember (and then only dimly) the vanished glory of those golden days when the power of Rome had both administered and protected the island province. Only an ageing and diminishing generation could boast of having seen the shining columns of infantry marching proudly along the straight roads, the burnished bronze of helmet and shield gleaming in the sunshine. The barracks lay empty, the forts were deserted; and from the silent stables of the cavalry the smell of polished leather and the acrid scent of horses had long since faded.

The great wall, which had been built in the first century by Hadrian to protect the province from the barbarians who dwelt in the inaccessible and mountainous forests of Caledonia, had long since lost its garrison. The triumphant Picts could now safely scale the deserted ramparts, could wander victoriously and yet in awe through the empty guardrooms and mess-halls of the vanished armies, and could then march south to harry the rich lands which they had so long coveted.

Yet, though Rome's presence was a long lifetime away, the Britons still looked to her as the exemplar of orderly government, and still hoped that the good days could be revived, with new

THE MAIN TRIBES OF PRE-ROMAN AND ROMAN BRITAIN

legions sailing to the island to protect them. They remembered the Roman practice of enlisting barbarian troops into their armies, offering them the chance of earning by service the land, the money and the arms that they would otherwise have seized as booty. Accordingly the Britons now invited a group of warriors from Germany to come to their assistance against the invading Picts.

Twenty-seven years later, these troops rebelled and, sending for reinforcements from their savage kinfolk in Germany, fought ruthlessly for possession of the island. There was a long and merciless war, and 100 years after the first coming of the barbarian soldiers, physical desolation and spiritual despair had spread throughout the land of Britain. The orchards and cornfields of Kent, in which so many Roman villas had once stood, had been wrested from the Britons and the region was now an Anglo-Saxon kingdom. The great Roman fort at Pevensey had been seized by the invaders and all the Britons who vainly defended it had been put to the sword. The south coast was overrun and the West Saxons had there set up their powerful kingdom. North of the Humber the invaders were tightening their grip. All this is recorded in the *Anglo-Saxon Chronicle*.

It was then, some time before 547, that a British monk named Gildas wrote a book entitled *De Excidio Britanniae* (*The Destruction of Britain*), a history of the island from the time of the Roman conquest to his own day. He also wrote a much longer work, the *Epistle*, in which he rebuked his countrymen for their sins, and for their lack of unity in the face of danger.

The first of these works, *The Destruction of Britain*, is the only account that has survived of Roman Britain, from the earliest times to her last sad overthrow, written by a Briton. It is the only written source of many of the stories with which we are familiar and we must ask how reliable a source it is.

To call the work a history is misleading. It is not a history in the formal sense of the word; nor did Gildas set out to be objective and to relate all the facts coolly and dispassionately. It was rather a tract for the times, and a piece of special and passionate pleading. It is patriotic and political by design, and facts are recounted only to point a moral and to support his argument. Gildas himself, in his preface, says so in clear terms. He writes that he decided not to describe the dangers undergone by Britain's extremely powerful soldiers (*fortissimorum militum*), but rather to recount the faults of those whose weakness had brought his country to its present state. He was deliberately recording the worst features of life in Britain: the ineffectiveness of her rulers, the disobedience of her people, and the vices of the age. Too many interpreters of Gildas have ignored the warning in his preface and have taken his selective and poetical account as an unskilful attempt to represent the whole truth. This is largely why the myth of the Britons being swiftly defeated by the more vigorous and resolute Anglo-Saxon invaders has been accepted as history. From this myth many others, known to be equally untrue, have flowed into and coloured the story of Britain. In fact, by the time of Gildas, 100 heroic years had passed, and the Britons were still holding out against the invaders in many parts of the island.

The book opens calmly enough with a geographical account of the island, mentions its two great rivers of Thames and Severn and the shining cities, many adorned with fortifications, walls and towers, offering (and Gildas now advances the main purpose of his book) fine means of defence—the implication being that these means were not adequately exploited by his countrymen.

Gildas then gives an account of the first days of the Roman occupation; he prefaces this section with a note on his sources. There were, he says, no actual British books or records available; either they had been burned in the fighting or they had been carried off by those who had fled as refugees to the Continent. (This is a vital piece of information and helps to establish Gildas as a unique voice of the Romano-British people.) Therefore, he tells us, he will use continental sources. He goes out of his way to paint the weaknesses rather than the bravery of his ancestors, when they were faced with the organised and armoured might of the Roman invaders, 500 years before. He curtly dismisses the resistance offered to the legions of Claudius, and when he comes to the rising of the British queen Boudicca, who in her swift and well-planned war (AD 61) destroyed three great cities and whose terrible resolution and efficiency nearly brought Roman rule to an end, he describes her army as mere 'crafty foxes'. Their defeat, which was brought about only after the Romans had called in reinforcements from the Continent, he describes as submission: 'they held out their hands, woman-like, to be manacled; so that it is a matter of proverbial derision, far and wide, that the Britons are neither strong in war nor faithful in peace'.

This is wholly unlike the account given by the Roman writers such as Tacitus upon whom he claimed to have drawn. If he could so distort well-documented events, there is no reason to believe that he did not similarly distort those stories for which he is sole witness. Throughout his narrative, therefore, those passages which emphasise the weakness, the disunity and the vices of his fellow countrymen may be looked upon with suspicion. The political purpose of his book must be kept in mind.

His preface gives one other valuable hint as to the reliability of his story. His acknowledgement that, for the period of the Roman occupation, he made use of continental authors, allows his version of events to be checked against their accounts. Such a check does not inspire confidence in his ability to produce a coherent and sequential narrative. For example, his account of the Roman conquest of Britain—fully described by Caesar, Tacitus, Dio and others—is compressed into one short paragraph, bereft of all detail. There is no mention of Caesar's two invasions, of the landing 100 years later of the expeditionary force under Aulus Plautius in the reign of Claudius, or of the heroism of the British leader Caractacus. A century of well-documented history, from Caesar to Nero, is compressed into one tangled and uninformative paragraph.

> For the Kings of the Romans, when they had obtained the government of the globe, all the bordering regions having been subjugated as well as the islands over against the east, and when they had established their great reputation for strength by their first peace with the Parthians, on the confines of India, by which deed wars ceased in the whole world, yet the lines of flame which they had lit could not be put out nor be contained by the tossing ocean in the west but, passing across the sea, came to this island with none to oppose them, and reduced to obedience the not merely unwarlike but the faithless people, not so much by fire and sword and warlike engines, as they did with other nations, but with mere menaces and threatening shows of judgement upon their faces, striking terror into their hearts.

This passage (the single sentence comprising chapter five of Gildas's book) is a good example of his method. The basic fact is accurate: 'The authorities in Rome, at a time when they had pacified the East, turned westwards, crossed the seas to Britain and swiftly conquered the island.' But his method of writing (he himself admitted that he had a 'vile style'—*vili licet stylo*) leaves the reader breathless and bewildered; the simple facts of the narrative are buried in the lush abundance of loquacity, and his contempt for his defeated ancestors hardly makes him the ideal historian. We have to learn to hack our way through the verbal jungle that seems to spring and burgeon magically from his pen, in order to discover the few facts hidden under all this disorganised exuberance.

Style apart, Gildas's story of Rome's conquest of Britain is so meagre that almost no reliance can be placed upon his claim to have referred to continental authors. Had he done so, at least one or two recognisable references from them might be expected, if not actual quotations; Gildas was perfectly capable of quoting extensively when he wished to do so. His other work, the *Epistle*, is full of passages from the Bible, carefully and appositely set in the text.

His account of events after the conquest is equally slight. He expresses the totality of the Roman occupation clearly and succinctly: 'It was not thought of as Britain but as the Roman Island; and whatsoever money it might possess—of bronze, silver or gold—was marked with the portrait of Caesar.' But of details there are none, and again his use of the sources from which he claimed to work is suspect.

In his account of Christianity in Britain during the Roman period, Gildas makes a statement which on the face of it could have supreme importance.

> Meanwhile these islands, stiff with freezing cold, and in distant lands by no means near to the visible sun, received the true sun, showing to the universal world its shining and coruscating light not merely from the temporal firmament but even from the height of the heavens, exceeding all temporal things; at the time, as we know, of the end of the reign of Tiberius Caesar.

Now Tiberius was emperor at the time of the Crucifixion so that Gildas is stating that Britain was brought Christianity in the days of the Apostles and was therefore one of the first lands to receive it. His story is circumstantial, for he adds that Tiberius not only permitted Christianity to flourish, but threatened death to all those who opposed it. The story is an attractive one, and it supports the legend of the coming of Joseph of Arimathea to Britain. For had Joseph visited Britain, it would indeed have been during the latter part of the reign of Tiberius. Gildas's phrase 'as we know' suggests that he and his contemporaries knew and believed the tale of Britain's early conversion; unfortunately it is supported by no other authority, and there is strong evidence to the contrary. Suetonius, Tiberius's biographer, specifically states that the emperor banned those foreign religions which had been adopted from the Egyptians and the Jews (and this included Christianity), treating them as mere superstitions. Moreover, the character of Tiberius in itself makes the story unlikely. On his favourite island of Capri he indulged in orgies which the modern mind finds difficult to believe and which even horrified his biographer. A man who decorated his home with pornographic pictures, and who vilely used babies for his obscene pleasures, is a dubious candidate for the position of pioneer supporter of Christianity! Reluctantly we must discard the story. We may speculate, however, that some Christians did come to Britain during his reign, leaving a memory and a tradition of which Gildas and his contemporaries had heard.

For events in Britain during the reign of Diocletian, Gildas is a better witness. This Emperor came to power towards the end of the third century AD and savagely persecuted the Christians in the early 300s, some 250 years before the time of Gildas. In describing these events, Gildas appears to have had access to good source material, for his account is coherent and detailed, giving full names of persons and places. He records the destruction of churches, the burning of copies of the Scriptures, the slaughter of the faithful, and the backsliding of those who could not face the fury and the torment. He hints at his source, mentioning that all these things were narrated in an ecclesiastical history—*ecclesiastica historia narrat*. Was there perhaps an *Ecclesiastical History of Britain* extant in his day, upon which he based this part of his work?

He names three martyrs, Aaron and Julius of the 'City of the Legion', and Alban of Verulamium. Alban's martyrdom is described in detail: how he changed clothes with a Christian fugitive, was arrested and condemned to death. A river had to be forded for him to reach his place of martyrdom and God parted the river (as he had once parted the Red Sea) so that Alban might cross dry-shod. Even when he had good material to work on, Gildas's grasp of detail is not impressive—he refers to the river as the Thames, though Verulamium, the modern St Albans, lies twenty miles and more north of it.

In 313 the Emperor Constantine issued the Edict of Milan, which recognised Christianity as a lawful religion and gave it the support and blessing of the Imperial government. Gildas states (the chronology shaky but not wildly out) that 'less than ten years' after the persecution of Diocletian, the followers of Christ, after the long winter's night, began to see again the kindly light of heaven. The churches that had been destroyed were rebuilt and new churches were founded in honour of the martyrs. (This passage suggests that the church at St Albans originated during that period; perhaps archaeology will one day support Gildas.)

There followed a period of dissension arising from the Arian heresy which Gildas describes in a characteristic passage. The members of the Church in Britain are likened to wild beasts, their jaws dripping with the poison of false beliefs, inflicting with their fangs terrible wounds upon their country 'which always wishes to hear some novelty or other and is stable in nothing'. Arius was a priest of Alexandria who, during the first quarter of the fourth century, argued that the Son could not be the eternal God in the same way as God the Father. For a while the Church was split and no doubt the schism spread to Britain. It would have given rise to long and intricate arguments as to the manner in which God the Son, though existing in all ages, was created by God the Father, but at least we can be sure that the Arians did not behave as ravening beasts! Once again Gildas gives the facts, but distorts and exaggerates them.

Gildas next describes the adventures of Maximus, the Spanish officer serving with the Roman army in Britain who won himself an immortal place in British folklore. He himself in 383 marched the Roman Legions stationed in Britain on Rome, conquered it, and was finally defeated and slain at Aquileia. Gildas's account of Maximus's vain and wasteful adventure is accurate, and so is his assessment of its outcome. Unlike later writers, Gildas does not view the ruthless and ambitious figure of Maximus with pride, rejoicing that the armies of Britain had captured the Eternal City, setting their leader upon the throne of the Caesars. He saw him rather as a tyrant, unlawfully bearing the imperial insignia. As a result, says Gildas, Britain was bereft of her soldiers and legions, and of all her youth who accompanied 'the aforesaid tyrant and never again returned'. Maximus left for his doomed adventure in 383, some 160 years before Gildas's time, so here the historian seems to be drawing on older material, using it critically and competently.

These events are described in chapter 13 of *The Destruction of Britain*; the next firm date appears in chapter 20, where reference is made to matters that occurred in 446. Everything described in chapters 14 to 20, then, must have occupied a period of sixty-three years—from 383 to 446. Assuming that here as elsewhere a few firm facts lie among the flourishes of rhetoric and the bitterness of sorrow, it is worth noting what is said of these dark years.

First, Gildas describes Britain's suffering 'for many years' from raids of the Picts from the north, and the Scots (possibly from Ireland) from the north-west. The Britons sent representatives to Rome to seek assistance. A legion was sent, and the barbarians were driven out of the province. This may well be authentic history, for after Maximus's disastrous adventure, Rome sent her great general Stilicho to Britain some time between 395 and 399. We know too that at this time Chrysanthus, a Christian, was sent to Britain as governor; he later became a bishop in Constantinople. Britain's hopes briefly revived as Stilicho defeated the invaders, made the seas safe and the land secure. Gildas adds—quite wrongly—that the legion built a wall across the island from sea to sea before sailing away. But this error of detail (no doubt a gratuitous addition by Gildas to the true tale which he had obtained from good sources) again does not invalidate his main narrative.

Stilicho left Britain in 402 to fight the Goths who, in eight more years, were to capture Rome itself and thus overthrow the Empire. Once he had gone, and taken his legion with him, the invaders renewed their attacks. Gildas speaks of seaborne invasions, of a breaking through of the frontiers and of widespread slaughter, and he states that the Britons again appealed to Rome. A combined force of sailors and cavalry was sent to the island, and in a brief and triumphant campaign, completely conquered the invaders, causing great destruction among them and driving the survivors back home to their own lands. For this second rescue, Gildas is the only witness. Though the first may perhaps be identified with the campaign of Stilicho, the second cannot be placed within the framework of known history. If Gildas is recording the truth (and, as we have seen, behind his rhetoric there often lurks a description of some factual event), then this second expedition was perhaps led by some local commander from Gaul, whose name was not well enough known to find a place in the continental chronicles, and who led a small but effective force to fight a purely local action.

When these troops left—the last Roman soldiers to visit Britain—Gildas says that the Britons were exhorted to take up arms and defend themselves; according to Zosimus, the Emperor Honorius in 410 sent a similar exhortation to the lost province. If Gildas's words represent a tradition based on the rescript of Honorius, taken not from written records but from an orally transmitted memory, then we have an approximate date for the second rescue; it must have taken place after the departure of Stilicho in 402 and before the rescript of Honorius in 410. In the same passage, however, Gildas records that it was now that the great wall was built, from sea to sea, by public and private contributions. This is clearly a reference to Hadrian's Wall, which was in fact built 200-300 years earlier. The Wall, all records lost and its origins forgotten, had to be explained, and the ascription of its building to this period was a reasonable guess; oral tradition and folk memories are rarely precise on detail, but may still be accurate on the central theme. From the facts available to Gildas, the story was at least plausible.

Immediately after the departure of the troops of the second rescue, Gildas claims that the Picts and Scots renewed their incursions both by sea and by land. These tribes differed in their customs, but were alike in their thirst for blood and in covering their faces with hair rather than their private parts with clothing—a remark which has prompted one modern historian (R. W. Chambers, *England Before the Norman Conquest*) to suggest that this is an early reference to the kilt! From this point onwards Gildas's narrative becomes far more coherent. If, as has been suggested (in Beram Saklatvala's *Arthur: Roman Britain's Last Champion*), Gildas was born in 517, he is now writing of a period a mere 100 years before his birth, for which oral tradition would have been strong and increasingly reliable. He records that the new wave of invaders rapidly seized all the northern parts of the country, after a vain attempt had been made to man Hadrian's Wall. The whole fabric of society was crumbling within the once-proud Roman province. The citizens were slaughtered mercilessly by the victorious barbarians or were put to flight, and had in their turn taken to plundering and robbery in order to survive. Internal dissension added to the disaster. Agriculture and the distribution of food broke down, and men relied upon hunting for their sustenance—like their remote and uncivilised ancestors. Order was fading, but it did not altogether vanish. A letter was sent to Aetius, one of Rome's greatest generals, who was now Consul in Rome (Gildas records) for the third time. We know that Aetius's third consulship was in 446, so that again Gildas's story can be dated. Thirty terrible years had passed since the exhortation of Honorius. They were years of defeat and slaughter, with armed bands of savages ranging over Britain, killing and plundering, with the once-rich owners of villas seeing their granaries empty and their workshops idle, and with frightened men leaving their houses and taking to the woods and hills. Yet somewhere in the island enough civilisation continued for the formal appeal to be sent to Aetius for a renewal of Rome's help. But the appeal was vain.

At about this time, the barbarians slackened their attacks, there was a good harvest and the country enjoyed an unprecedented but all-too-brief period of prosperity. Then (and remembering Gildas's political purpose allowances have to be made), the people turned to luxury and civil war, to fornication and all manner of crimes. Also, it seems, there was schism, for Gildas writes angrily of men denying truth, venerating evil instead of good, and accepting Satan as an angel of light. Kings were anointed because they excelled in cruelty.

For all his tale of unrelieved viciousness and gloom, Gildas unwittingly implies that civilisation continued, government survived, and Roman order and methods were remembered. For all the counsellors of the nation, at one with 'that proud tyrant Guerthrigernus', invited the Saxons to the island 'to repel the invasions of the northern nations'. Guerthrigernus is of course the King Vortigern of history, and he was doing no more than following standard Roman practice. (Aetius himself had done the same on the Continent: he had defeated the Burgundians who were seeking to destroy Roman Gaul and they were later invited by the authorities to settle in the province as allies.) To Gildas, writing 100 years later, when the Saxons and their allies had seized almost the entire province, shattering all that Gildas valued of the old days of Roman rule and Christian culture, Vortigern's actions were unforgivable. From his decision to call in the Saxons there had flowed the total destruction of generations of civilised existence.

To trace the story in the pages of Gildas is to hear the living voice of the despairing Britons. Vortigern and his counsellors were blind, they were inviting wolves into the sheepfold. No other event in history had been so harmful to the country, nor more unlucky. The emotions ring true as does the narrative itself. To begin with, the new allies, together with the reinforcements they summoned from their own land, were content to give good service in return for the supplies they received. But then they demanded more and more, threatening to break the treaty if their demands were not met. Break the treaty they did: they swept the island like fire, burning churches, destroying cities and towns. The stones of broken walls and of smashed altars, fragments of human bodies together with the ruins of broken towers, lay in the streets of the sacked towns. The dead were left to rot in the deserted houses, and wild animals and birds feasted on the neglected corpses.

Then Britain found a saviour in Ambrosius Aurelianus, described as being of Roman descent and background. His successors were still fighting when Gildas wrote *The Destruction of Britain.* The great battle of Mount Badonicus was the triumphant climax of the Britons' resistance, and was fought in 517, Gildas tells us, the year that he was born. The Saxons suffered tremendous slaughter, and it was followed by a period of great happiness for the Britons. The old vices ceased and all men returned to the ways of duty and virtue. But the generation which had seen the vicissitudes of the Saxon attacks, as well as the miracle of the great victory, died. And with them died the memories of past sorrows and the unexpected blessing. With them, too, died piety, justice and duty; and Gildas ends his book with a description of his countrymen rushing headlong into hell—demoralised, divided and despairing.

His second work, the *Epistle*, is much longer and much less informative. It opens with a terrible indictment of the kings and judges of Britain; the kings were tyrants, the judges unrighteous. They protected evil men, they lied, they despised the humble and the innocent.

Gildas rebukes several kings by name. Constantine, King of Devon and Cornwall, disguised as an abbot, had foully murdered two young princes at prayer in a church; he divorced his wife and followed the sins of Sodom. Aurelius Conanus was a murderer and an adulterer, and promoted civil war. Vortipore lay with his daughter; and Cuneglass—'the yellow butcher'—once drove the chariot of the man known as the Bear. He, too, had divorced his wife and had then married her sister—a nun. Maglocunus, 'soaked in the wine of the sodomitical grape', as a young man had rebelled against his uncle the king, whom he destroyed with all his army. Later, Maglocunus became a monk, only to return 'like a dog to his vomit' to his former life of violence and sin. He had divorced and later murdered his wife, marrying the widow of a nephew whom he also murdered.

All these kings of the different provinces in Britain were contemporaries of Gildas, so that his stories, while exaggerated, are probably substantially true. A glimpse of the chaos in Britain is conveyed—cut off from Rome, beset by pagan enemies, with many of her regions already in Saxon hands. Order and decency were no more, and many of the kings of Britain, oblivious of the mortal peril in which their country stood, were concerned only with their immediate ambitions and conquests. None of those listed by Gildas appears to have been conscious of the urgent need to defend, together with their fellow kings, the land in which they reigned and held their illusory power. It is one of the local kings in Britain, Maglocunus, who gives a date for Gildas's work: he died, as we shall see, in 547, so that the book must have been written before that date.

The rest of the *Epistle* contains little or no historical material. It is rather a collection of sermons, angrily delivered to a heedless and degenerate people. Gildas summons as his witnesses Samuel, the founder of a lawful and holy kingdom; David the hero king; Jeroboam and Baasha, the two blaspheming monarchs of Israel; Hosea and Amos, Micah and Ezekiel. He recalls the prophecies of Isaiah and Jeremiah, quoting the latter on the theme of foolish people and cruel kings. For the unrighteous there is destruction—fire, sword and the anger of God. He quotes Amos's threats to the sons of Judah who had cast away God's law—God would send fire upon Judah and destroy the foundations of Jerusalem.

He could foretell, not merely with the frenzy of a prophet, but with the sense of doom of the historian, how the tragedies of the Old Testament would be repeated in Britain; and how the Britons would no more survive against their enemies than did the Jews, driven as fugitives from their country and scattered over a hostile world. There were none, he recorded, willing to suffer for the truth or to defy the unrighteous, as did the martyrs of apostolic times. He recalled Christ's words to Peter: 'Thou art Peter, and upon this rock I will build my Church.' But also he quotes the harsher words: 'Depart from me, all ye workers of iniquity.'

The kings had failed and the soldiers had fought and fallen in vain. Roman Britain was dead, murdered by the bloody and remorseless hands of the Saxons helped by the weakness of the Britons themselves. It was for the priests to be like Peter, firm rocks upon which the faith might be built and endure. In the event, the passionate prayers of Gildas were answered. For the Church of the Britons did indeed survive; priests and monks continued their work for another 100 years and more, preserving the faith in mountains and valleys in the far west of their island. They lost their land but retained their firm faith and their ancient identity, living on to this day in the defiant hills of Wales.

What kind of man was Gildas and what were the experiences, both at home and abroad, that gave him his burning patriotism, his anger against his fellow countryman, and his deep sense of foreboding that Roman Britain, of which he was so much a part, had reached the tragic end of her story?

Two Latin biographies of him have survived, one probably written in the eleventh century and one in the twelfth, some six or seven hundred years after his death. The earlier manuscript is entiled *Vita Gildae, auctore monacho Ruyensi anonyme* (*The Life of Gildas* by an unnamed monk of Ruys); the second biography (of which there are two manuscripts, both in the British Museum) is said to have been written by Caradoc of Llancarfan. The name of Caradoc appears on the Royal MS (13 B.VII), which was written at about the time of Henry VIII's reign. This is too late a date for us to be quite sure, but Caradoc's authorship is generally accepted.

Between Caradoc's biography and that by the anonymous monk there are many discrepancies. Some have therefore said that there were two men named Gildas, alive at different times. This argument was first advanced by Archbishop Usher in the seventeenth century. The Archbishop had a passion for chronology, and his precise dating of events, both historical and legendary (not excluding the creation itself) is well known. The solution he proposed is advanced in modern reference books, for example in the *Encyclopaedia Britannica*.

The contradictions between the two works, however, are no more than might be expected when one remembers that the two biographies were written in different countries, at different periods, and were probably based on two different sources and traditions. Both, moreover, were composed five or six centuries after the events described. The hard facts available to each writer would have been few, and both would have added to these the products of their own devout minds. As significant as the differences are the many points where the two narratives agree. Both report that Gildas was born in Scotland. In Caradoc's version his father is called Nau, in the other Cau. Caradoc makes him the brother of Hueil, while the other writer makes him the son of Cuil. Both have stories about a bell. Both speak of Gildas's stay in Ireland and of his visit to Rome.

As to the internal discrepancies within each biography, we must remember that medieval authors who wrote the lives of the saints were more concerned with piety than with accuracy. They knew that their readers expected that the stories should have an accustomed and familiar shape, with miraculous episodes, and deep devotion on the part of the hero. Authors had to satisfy the avid credulity of their readers rather than try to defend themselves cautiously against severe and critical scholarship.

The *Life* written by Caradoc is brief, and would occupy barely ten pages of a modern printed book. It tells us that among the noblest of the kings of Scotland was a man named Nau, who had twenty-four warlike and victorious sons. One was called Gildas and his parents set him to the study of literature. When still a young man he crossed the channel to Gaul where he studied for seven years. He returned to Britain with a huge and varied collection of books. His fame spread and numerous scholars flocked to him, many of whom later became officers of state. He was the wisest of all the teachers of religion in Britain, and no one could equal him.

As to his personal character, we are told that he fasted like a hermit, prayed continually and gave to the poor whatever was given to him. He abstained from sweet milk and honey, holding things of the flesh in contempt. He ate simply, drank spring water and never entered the baths to which the Britons were then greatly addicted. His face was thin and he appeared to suffer from fever. He would stand in a cold river at midnight and pray until the dawn came. He slept on a stone floor with only one covering.

There were three kingdoms in Britain, and the kings feared and obeyed him and listened to his preaching. Nemata, the mother of St David, came to hear him during her pregnancy before David was born. Gildas found that he could not continue preaching. An angel explained to him that Nemata was in the church, that she was pregnant, and that she was a woman of exceeding grace. But her future son would be of even greater grace. In her presence, therefore, he could not preach.

Later, Gildas crossed to Ireland where he converted innumerable people to the faith. He was a contemporary of Arthur, king of all Greater Britain, whom he greatly loved and respected. His brother however resisted the rebel king, not wishing to be Arthur's subject. While Gildas was studying in Ireland the news came to him that his elder brother Hueil (*belliger assiduus et miles famomissimus*—'an assiduous warrior and most famous soldier') had been killed by King Arthur. He wept at the news and thereafter prayed daily for his brother's soul, whereas before he had prayed for Arthur, his brother's killer.

Then Gildas came back to Britain bringing with him a most beautiful and sweet-sounding bell, which was received by the Venerable Abbot of Llancarfan. News of his return came to King Arthur and to all the leading bishops and abbots in Britain. Peace was made between Gildas and Arthur, and sealed with a kiss. Arthur, weeping, accepted the penance laid upon him by the bishops.

Later, Gildas travelled to Rome, taking the bell with him as an offering to the Church of St Peter; but when the Pope shook it, the bell made no sound. The Pope, who knew the Abbot of Llancarfan, took the bell's silence as a miraculous sign that the gift ought to be returned to Llancarfan, and this was done. Whoever swore a false oath by this bell would suffer.

On his return, Gildas was invited by Cadoc, Abbot of Llancarfan, to spend a year supervising the students. While there he wrote a work on the four Evangelists, decorated with gold and silver, which, the writer tells us, was still at Llancarfan in his own day and was considered most sacred for the taking of oaths.

When the year was over, both Abbot Cadoc and Gildas withdrew from Llancarfan to two islands, Ronech and Echin—the Abbot to the one nearer Wales and Gildas to the one nearer England. Gildas founded an oratory in honour of the Holy and Undivided Trinity, close to which he set up his own cell. He did not place his bed inside, but would lie beneath a high rock until midnight, praying; then, freezing, he would return to his church. He caught small fish in a net and took eggs from the nests of wild birds, and this was sufficient food for him. The two men visited each other from time to time, and so lived for seven years.

The Creator, seeing his beloved servant Gildas drenched by raindrops which fell upon the stones, made a river flow from the high rock, and it still flows without cease. Then, while Gildas continued intently praying and fasting, pirates from the Orkney Islands seized the servants who waited upon him and carried them off into exile with all the booty they could find. Gildas left his island and went with great sorrow to Glastonbury, at the time that King Meluas reigned *in aestiva regione*—in the summer region (Somerset). (*Glastonia*, the Glass City, was named *Ynniswitrin* or Glass Island in the British tongue.) He was welcomed by the Abbot of Glastonbury and, Caradoc relates, there taught the monks and many of the common people, sowing the seed of the heavenly doctrine. There he wrote his histories of the kings of Britain. Then Glastonbury was besieged by Arthur 'the tyrant' with a large army on account of Guennuar his wife, who had been violated and carried off by the evil King Meluas, and taken to Glastonbury, which was well protected by rivers and marshes. Arthur had sought his queen for a year, and marched on Glastonbury with the armies of *Cornubia* and *Dibuenia* (Cornwall and Devon); everything was ready for war.

Seeing this, the Abbot of Glastonbury—accompanied by Gildas—went between the armies and advised King Meluas to make peace and give up Guennuar. This he did, the two kings made gifts of land to the abbey, and visited the Church of St Mary to pray there. At peace, they left promising to obey the Abbot and never again to violate that most holy spot nor any of the land near by.

Gildas now longed to return to the life of a hermit; on the banks of a river close to Glastonbury he again built a church in the name of the Holy and Undivided Trinity. In this church he fasted and prayed assiduously, giving all men an example of a virtuous and religious life. Pilgrims visited him from the most distant parts of Britain, and listened with joy to his advice and exhortations.

At length he fell sick and called the Abbot of Glastonbury who begged him piously, now that his life was ending, to bequeath his body to the Abbey of Glastonbury which he loved so much. Then, amid grief and tears, the most holy Gildas expired, and many saw an angelic splendour shining around his body, and about him hung the odour of sanctity; and they saw angels accompanying his soul. His body was carried by his brother monks to the Abbey and buried with great honour beneath the floor in the middle of the Church of St Mary. 'And his soul' concludes the author of the *Life* 'found rest, and rests still, and shall continue to rest, in heavenly rest.'

How much of the true facts of Gildas's life can be gathered from this work?

The first point to be made is that no dates are given. One event, his visit to Rome, would have helped in the task of dating if the author had given the name of the Pope whom Gildas saw, but unfortunately he is referred to merely as *apostolicus*, the apostolic one. Indeed, the absence of the Pope's name does not merely deny us a date, but must cast some doubt upon the authenticity of the tale. If the visit had in fact been made, and if it had been noted in some contemporary record to which Caradoc had had access, such an important detail as the Pope's name would scarcely have been omitted. Against this, the visit is also mentioned by the other biographer, the anonymous monk of Ruys. Whether or not Gildas went to the Eternal City, the story of the silent bell must be assigned to the area of pious legend.

Only two points in the story can help with dates. First is the reference to the presence of St David's mother, Nemata, in the church where Gildas was preaching. In this context the truth of Caradoc's tale can be checked against other evidence, for much is known about St David, a biography of whom was written by Rhygyrarch in the eleventh century. First, his mother's name is given as Non, which may justify the speculation that both derive from a common and older tradition.

We know too that St David, while Archbishop in Caerleon, presided there over an assembly of bishops which became known as the Synod of Victory. The date of this meeting was 569 (according to the *Annales Cambriae*), and we also know that St David died in 601, thirty-two years later. We have no date for his birth, but assuming that he was thirty or forty when he became Archbishop, he would have been born in about 530-40, and would have been sixty or seventy when he died. Gildas himself was probably born in 517 (dying in 570), so the two were certainly contemporaries. Indeed, if we take 540 as the date of St David's birth, Gildas would have been in his twenties, and the story that he met David's mother just before her son was born is not impossible. The account of the incident, therefore (whatever our opinion may be of the miracle itself) goes to support the authenticity of at least this part of the *Life* and, in passing, helps to fix a possible date for the birth of St David. It is also consistent with the date (517) inferred from Gildas's own writings as to the year of his own birth. (See page 30.)

The other sections of the *Life* which help in establishing a chronological scale are the references to Arthur and the specific statement that Gildas was his contemporary—*contemporeanus Gildas vir sanctissimus fuit Arturi regis totius Majoris Brittaniae* (Gildas was a contemporary of Arthur, king of all Great Britain.) Here we are on firmer ground. A good chronicle, the *Annales Cambriae* (to be considered later), gives 537 as the date of Arthur's death and, as we have seen, Gildas died in 570. On this point therefore the narrative rings true. Moreover the references to Arthur are such as to suggest that Caradoc has drawn on very old material, possibly contemporary with the events of the story. Twice he describes Arthur as *rex rebellis*, and once as *Arturus tyrannus*. By the twelfth century, when the *Life* was written, the legends about Arthur were becoming established. In the works of Geoffrey of Monmouth, a contemporary of Caradoc of Llancarfan, Arthur had become a great hero of whom many marvels were told and whose virtues were as outstanding as his prowess. The description of him as a rebel king and as a tyrant does not match the concept of him then current, and therefore almost certainly derives from documents of a far earlier age, before the legends had obscured the truth, and when Arthur was still being judged by men familiar with both the good and the evil of his life. The words used in the *Life* suggest that the sources which Caradoc used had adopted the judgement made by Arthur's enemies. Arthur, we must remember, died in a civil war, and passages in the *Life* argue strongly that, for matters concerning him, Caradoc had available a written document originally composed shortly after Arthur's death in 537. The references, moreover, make the broad chronology of the work consistent with the dates for Gildas which we shall consider from the latter's own works. They give general support to the authenticity of the *Life* as a whole and to that of the account of Arthur in particular.

It is impossible to distinguish with certainty, however, between the hard facts and the decorative features added by Caradoc or the earlier writers upon whose work he drew. We are only justified in accepting that Gildas came into contact with Arthur and was almost certainly in conflict with him. Arthur had many opponents in Britain. The epithets used by Caradoc make it clear that the account which he used, written by an admirer of Gildas, was written by one who considered Arthur a rebel and a tyrant. This would seem to place Gildas himself firmly in the anti-Arthur party, who remembered the Saint as a holy protagonist of their own cause. We may also accept that Arthur had some contact with Glastonbury, though not the detailed story of the evil King Meluas, nor the account of the siege. Finally, the name of Arthur's wife, Guennuar, supports other legends and suggests her traditional name of Guinevere is not too wide of the mark.

In other parts of the narrative inaccuracies are apparent. Caradoc states, for example, that there were three kingdoms in Britain. But Gildas himself in his *Epistle* vehemently rebukes no fewer than four kings by name. Those whom he addresses are parricides, adulterers and totally iniquitous. Presumably there were others, rather more virtuous, whom he did not mention. Caradoc's inaccuracy on this detail may be due to nothing more than the Welsh love of the magical figure three, so frequently encountered in legend and history. What follows, however, is almost certainly true. The kings in Britain must have feared the harsh-tongued and stormy monk, hurling the thunder of his invective and the lightning of his contempt at those whom he felt had failed in their duty, and not hesitating to describe them as 'tyrants not kings'.

The description of Gildas's extreme asceticism, of the relentless manner in which he mortified his flesh, may contain some genuine tradition. True, it is twice repeated, once in the early part of the work and again in the account of his behaviour in his island hermitage. The reiteration is a little unconvincing, since Caradoc may be repeating a mere formula, not describing Gildas individually but drawing a stereotyped and standard portrait of a holy man. Yet when allowance has been made for the piety of the biographer and the standards of his times, the two passages seem to ring true. Gildas in his own works appears as a highly emotional man, subject to the storms of inner passion and to hurricanes of anger. In one who possessed a passionate nature, but whose vocation and convictions alike demanded a contempt for all passion, self-mortification and the harsh disciplining of his own flesh would have been the natural counterpart of a harsh and almost hysterical denunciation of the sins of other men.

So we may deduce a few uncertain facts. We can accept that Gildas was born in the north, of noble lineage, and that he had several brothers. After becoming a monk and after many years of study, he crossed into Ireland. If the Nemata story is true, and if the events set down in Caradoc's *Life* are in chronological order, this would have been some time after 540, the year of David's birth. This cannot be reconciled with the statement that Arthur slew Hueil while Gildas was in Ireland, for Arthur died in battle in 537. We must, therefore, assume that Caradoc, in writing down the separate tales that he had collected about Gildas, did not arrange them in strict chronological order.

Thus the general portrait of Gildas is fairly clear, despite the impossibility of discovering the facts of his life in detail. Learned and devoted, with a deep and detailed knowledge of the Scriptures, he was a man in whom religion had wrought a deep and abiding change. Known as Gildas the Wise, generations of historians and chroniclers quoted him as a high authority. A gaunt ascetic figure, thin of face and vehement in all he did, he mortified his own flesh as relentlessly as he castigated the sins of the flesh in others. He feared God but was afraid of no man, not even of the tyrannical kings of Britain. The sternness of the Old Testament made a deeper appeal to him than the tenderness of the New. Yet he was able to make his peace with his brother's slayer, disciplining his anger as he had learned to discipline his body and its passions. Against his fellow-countrymen and their weaknesses he was filled with wrath—a wrath which his pen has made immortal.

He is the only direct witness of the tragic days when Roman Britain, mauled by her last and triumphant enemies, lay dying. For events in the later years of Roman Britain's collapse—events which he himself saw—his testimony must be accepted. Through all his rhetoric and anger, he takes us back vividly both to the events and emotions of that muddled, savage period. He wrote to rouse his people to resolution and virtue. In this he failed. But he succeeded in making us hear, in a real and individual voice, in tones harsh with anger and broken with despair, the sorrows and perils of those mournful years.

II

THE WELSH ANNALS AND THE CHRONICLE OF THE PRINCES OF WALES

WITHIN twenty or thirty years of Gildas's death in 570, his prophecies of woe had been tragically fulfilled. The Britons had now lost the long and stubborn war which, for 150 years, they had been waging against the Germanic invaders. The latter were now in firm possession of almost the whole of the former Roman province. Many of the Britons lived on in the new English kingdoms that had now been set up. But there they were, at best, second-class citizens (new laws set a lower value upon them than upon their English counterparts) and, at worst, slaves.

Their descendants continued to dwell in the cities and farms of England, at first conscious of their separate and defeated identity. As the centuries passed, time wore away their proud memories of former power and the bitter resentment of their loss. Intermarriage with their former enemies and the facing of common dangers from foreign intruders brought the two peoples slowly together, so that today in England itself Celt and Saxon are one. For many generations the defeated Britons, sullen but defiant, with ancient anger their guide and with inextinguishable hope the beacon that signalled them to war, maintained their own kingdoms in Devon and Cornwall, and in some parts of the north. Here, as we shall see, they fought on for many years, allying themselves with English kings if by so doing they could inflict harm or mischief upon the general English cause.

But it was only in the wild lands of Wales, whose hills and towering mountains gave pause to the Saxons for a further six centuries, that the Britons survived as a nation. Here they lived, and live to this day, with the immortal memories of their vanished greatness, speaking a version of the language they spoke when the legions marched past their neat farms and towns, and remembering their dead heroes. Here they buried in their hearts the treasure of their ancient and unique heritage. And here they nursed, and kept alive from generation to unforgiving generation, a bitter resentment of their cruel dispossession.

In Wales they kept their Christian faith, which had come to them in Roman times. Monasteries flourished and in those monasteries learning survived. In growing isolation from both the military and ecclesiastical power of Rome, the tenacious Britons clung obstinately to the institutions they had inherited. Bishops were appointed, synods were held, and civilisation somehow continued in the face of disaster. And so that the memory of great events might not perish, nor the names of great men be forgotten, records were written and preserved in some of the monasteries.

One such record, the *Annales Cambriae* or the *Welsh Annals*, has survived. The copies we have (and there are only three manuscripts) were made much later than the first events to be noted. The earliest copy (known as Manuscript A) is in the Harleian collection in the British Museum. It is neatly written on parchment, set out in three columns, and the script is that of the late tenth or early eleventh century. This is the master copy and almost certainly represents the original version of the *Annals*. The first date entered is 444 and the entries go on more or less continually to the year 954. After this there are twenty-three blank years and the manuscript ends at 977. It must therefore have been copied from a version completed in the tenth century; even the later portions of that version were thus (on the evidence of the handwriting) some 200 years old when Manuscript A was made. This may well have been the last of many copies, with new ones being made from century to century as the older versions faded.

The second surviving copy (Manuscript B) is written—also in triple columns—on some of the flyleaves of an abridged copy of *Domesday Book* in the Public Record Office. This copy contains entries (beginning with the Creation) earlier than those in Manuscript A, and derived from a quite different source (Isidore's *Origines*); the chronology is totally unreliable. From about the period when Manuscript A begins, however, the two copies agree closely, though B loses seven years by 954. It continues thereafter until the early part of the thirteenth century.

The third copy (Manuscript C) is in the Cottonian collection in the British Museum and is basically similar to Manuscript B until the year 1203, after which it has fewer and fewer entries on Welsh affairs and becomes more and more an English document.

The form of the *Welsh Annals* is very simple. As a modern diary gives space for each day's events, so the pages of the *Annals* were marked off to provide a space for each year, beginning at 444. Each space is headed *Annus* (year) and every tenth year is numbered serially, so that the dates can be calculated from the initial entry of 444. For the most part, one brief Latin sentence suffices to describe each year's events, and many of the years have no entries at all. Since many of the entries deal with the deaths of saints and bishops, with battles and the deeds of kings, it is to be expected that in some years no events considered sufficiently noteworthy occurred. Neverthelesss, the number of omissions is significant and may help us in assessing which entries were contemporary accounts and in reaching tentative conclusions about the dates at which various sections of the document were written.

It is, for example, very striking that for the first fifty years (covering the period 444-96) there are only six entries, and for the next fifty years only five. It is hard to imagine that there would have been so few entries had these been the years when the record was begun. A chronicler conceiving a contemporary record of yearly events would surely have found something to fill out the first few years of his story, to maintain, as far as possible, the shape of what he had planned. The inference is that the work was drawn up many years after the dates of events described in the first entries. The first compiler was content to set down merely what he could learn from earlier documents or traditions, leaving the blank years unfilled; at least the form of the work would be established, and an example of a regular annual record be given his successors.

What prompted the man who began the *Annals* to take 444 as his starting date? Gildas, as we have seen, records that the Britons made their final appeal to Rome in the year when Aetius was Consul for the third time, that is to say in 446. By then the British cause seemed almost lost. In the words of their own message to Aetius, they were faced with the grim alternatives of having their throats cut by the barbarians or of drowning in the sea—their only refuge. The tone of their appeal was desperate, and desperate were the measures they took when it was unsuccessful, calling into their service the warlike Saxons by whom they had in the past been so savagely beset. They could not have reached so terrible a pass unless their armies had earlier suffered some massive and final defeat at the hands of the Picts and Scots. This great disaster could well have occurred in 444, and the initiator of the *Annals* might thus with some reason have selected this date, although the absence of any entry in the *Annals* for the first year to be inscribed upon its pages is certainly mysterious.

For the fifty years between 544 and 594 there are twelve completed entries, more than for the first two periods of fifty years taken together. It may be that this was the time when the *Annals* were first drawn up and the earlier entries collected from past records. This kind of dating would fit in with what we know of the period generally. The Battle of Mount Badonicus was described by Gildas as a great victory won by the Romanised Britons against the invading Saxons; it was probably fought in 517 and was succeeded by a long period of peace, a golden age lasting for a whole generation when men returned to piety and duty. Earlier, the times had been too troubled for the maintenance of full records; Gildas himself mentions in his preface that no British documents were available to him. This again suggests that the *Annals* were begun some time after he had written his own work, giving us a date after 547 for their commencement.

The first entry (which appears only in Manuscript B) is for the fourth year on the first page, 448, and reads *Dies tenebrosa sicut nox*, 'A day as shadowy as if it were night'. We know an eclipse of the sun was visible in Britain on 23 December 447, and the apparent difference of a year can be explained by differences in the date taken for New Year's day. The next entry, 453, is also accurate, recording that in that year 'Easter was changed to Sunday with the advice of Pope Leo, Bishop of Rome'. It was indeed in 453 that a dispute arose between the western church centred on Rome and the eastern church based on Constantinople, as to whether Easter, 455, should be celebrated on 17 or 24 April; Pope Leo finally assented to the computation of the eastern church. It is not strictly accurate to say that 'Easter was changed to Sunday', for the Church of Rome had celebrated Easter Sunday since the second century, but the establishment of a date for Easter by Pope Leo is a fact, and the *Annals* ascribe it to the correct year.

Under 547 is the entry: 'The great mortality in which died Mailcun, King of Guenedota.' The Great Plague, which spread from Western Asia, is known to have been rife in south-east Europe in 543-44. It could well have reached Britain by 547. The entry is of great significance in another context. For 'Mailcun, King of Guenedota' is of course King Maglocunus of Gwynnedd whom Gildas so bitterly rebuked as 'the dragon of the island'; he had seized the lands of many other kings, was a tall man, great in power, and practised the sins of Sodom. Gildas had addressed him directly, calling him to repentance and to God's service. Maglocunus was clearly very much alive at the time Gildas's

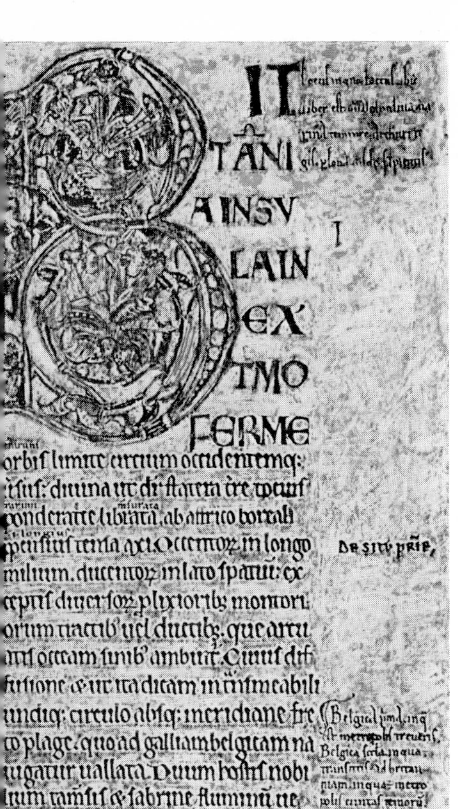

Page 49 (*left*):
Page from a late twelfth-century manuscript of the works of Gildas. Key, page 200.

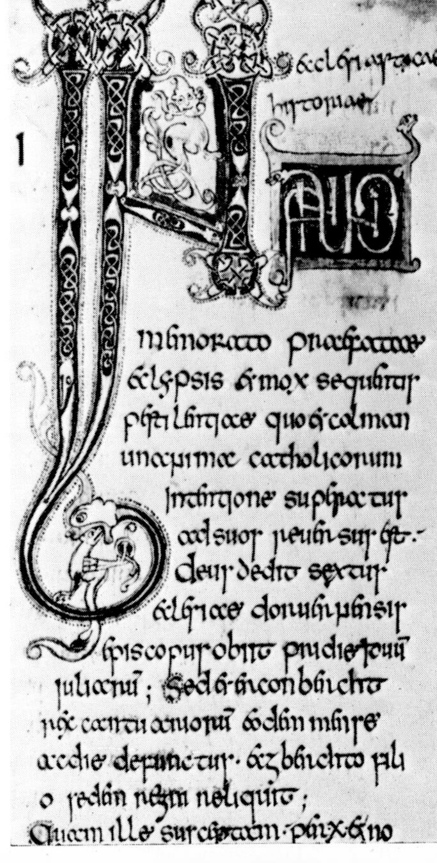

(*right*)
Page from a late eighth-century manuscript of Bede's *Historia Ecclesiastica Gentis Anglorum*. Key, page 200.

Page 50: Page from the most important manuscript of the *Annales Cambriae*.
Key, page 201.

words were written, so that the record in the *Annals* of the year of his death provides good evidence that Gildas's history was written before 547.

There are two direct references to Gildas in the *Annals*. In the year 565 'the journey of Gildas to Ireland' is recorded. The second reference is against the year 570: 'Gildas died.' In this entry, one of the manuscripts refers to Gildas as *sapiens*, the wise; another as *Britonum sapientissimus*, wisest of the Britons. One other entry, though not referring to Gildas by name, records an event mentioned by him. Against the year 516* appears a sentence far longer and fuller than any of the other items in this section of the work:

> The Battle of Badon in which Arthur carried the cross of our Lord Jesus Christ for three days and three nights on his shoulders, and the Britons were the victors.

This is evidently the same as the Battle of Mount Badonicus of Gildas and much can be learned from the entry. First, it records what Gildas omits, that the name of the victor was Arthur. Second, Arthur is not given the title of king as he is in Caradoc's *Life* of Gildas. Third, Arthur is shown as a Christian, carrying a Christian emblem.

The figure of Arthur emerges once more from the shadows in the entry of 537:

> Battle of Camlann in which Arthur and Medraut died and there was a plague in Britain and in Ireland.

The first word of this sentence is not *bellum*, a battle, as in the Mount Badonicus entry, but *gueith*, which is the British word for battle. In modern Welsh (particularly in the written language) the word is *cad* and it still means a battle. The use of *gueith* therefore suggests either that the account of the battle—whatever the year it was actually written down in the *Annals*—dates from the same period as the battle itself, or that it is derived

* Possibly in fact 517—see Saklatvala's *Arthur: Roman Britain's Last Champion*

from oral tradition. The great victory would have been on all men's lips and would have been spoken of as *Gueith Camlann*, a phrase that became 'familiar in their mouths as household words', and one that even a scholarly monk, writing in Latin, found it unnecessary to translate.

Camlann is of course the Camlan of the legends and Medraut is Mordred. The *Annals* and the legend support each other. Manuscript B adds a phrase which brings the legend and the *Annals* still further together:

> The Battle of Camlam, in which the famous Arthur, King of the Britons, and Modred his betrayer, died of the wounds they inflicted upon one another.

Note that the place where the battle was fought has become Camlam, a good example of the twists and turns that can stem from a slip of the copyist's pen. Arthur himself has become a king and the adjective used to describe him (*inclytus*—famous) is the same as that in the epitaph engraved on the coffin said to have been found at Glastonbury towards the end of the twelfth century. The coffin and the inscription are certainly later than Arthur's day and may well be spurious. To find the same epithet in this addition to the *Annals*, to find the Medraut of the main version changed to Mordred and thus nearer to the name of the legend, and to find Arthur not slain outright, but dying of his wounds as in the legends, all these must cast doubt on the antiquity of this additional sentence. It may well have been added when the copy was made, in order to bring the terse original text into line with what was now coming to be believed of Arthur. It is significant that the copy was made at about the same time as the discovery of the Glastonbury 'burial'.

One or two other early entries are worth examining in detail. In the year 501 'Bishop Ebur died in Christ in the three hundred and fiftieth year of his age'. The extraordinary longevity of this bishop is as suspicious as his name! More than 180 years earlier, three British bishops attended a council at Arles in Gaul. The name of one of them is shown in the sixth or seventh Corbie Codex as 'Eborius' from the city of York. This is almost certainly a confusion between the name of the See (*Eboracum*—York) and that of the bishop himself. The document in which the blunder was made was drawn up in the sixth or seventh century, not too long after the above entry. Has the blunder been repeated here? Are the *Annals* telling us that a British Bishop of York died in that year? This is quite possible, for the city was still in the hands of the Christian Britons in the seventh century—we know from Bede that it was at that time the capital of Caedwalla their king. In 501, then, it might well have been a Christian city, proud of its ancient past, and still defying the forces of heathendom which now held much of the country. If this is so, then the improbable age of the bishop might well have another meaning. It could be the age, real or reputed, of the See of York. True, this would give a date of AD 151 for the appointment of the first bishop, but there were many stories, today discredited, of the very early foundation of the Church in Britain. The date agrees remarkably well, for example, with the date given by Bede for the first conversion of Britain, AD 156. The tale of this conversion is no longer believed, but obviously it was once current. The 350th anniversary of the foundation of the See of York would have been a notable event, and would surely have found a place in the chronicles in the context of the death of the city's bishop in the same year. Certainly this interpretation, speculative though it is, seems more plausible than that a bishop (tough as Yorkshiremen are) lived to the age of 350!

For the year 573 is recorded the Battle of Armterid between two British leaders, Elifer and Guendolen, in which the latter fell. The golden age that followed Badon was now over, and the Britons were resuming their suicidal civil wars of which Gildas had so bitterly and despairingly complained. In the same year, we are told, tantalisingly and briefly, 'Merlin became insane'. This is thirty-three years after Arthur's death, and Merlin, if he were indeed Arthur's counsellor as the legends allege, must by now have been extremely old. He had seen his once victorious commander killed at Camlan in civil war, had seen the cause of Christianity defeated, and the heathen English almost everywhere triumphant. Perhaps the entry is trying to tell us of an old man, worn out by disappointment and despair, broken in mind as well as in body, in a last sad decline before he received the mercy of death.

A remarkable feature of the *Annals* is that during the whole of the first 150 years there is not one single reference to the Anglo-Saxon invaders, nor to the new English kingdoms being set up in the lost lands of the Britons. Yet these were the years when the bitter struggle was at its height. All the south had been overrun. An entire British army had been destroyed in the Roman fort of Anderida, the modern Pevensey. The West Saxons had founded their powerful kingdom across the southern strip of the once Roman island. The midlands had fallen and the kings of Mercia now ruled there. Along the east coast and north of the Humber the Angles had dispossessed the heirs of Rome and had organised their pagan and military kingdoms. Yet on all these matters the *Annals* are silent. True, the Battle of Badon is recorded, with the name of the British leader, Arthur. But there is no mention of his adversaries. Were it not for other sources (Gildas for example), we would not know whether Arthur's battle was fought against the proud invaders or whether it had been an engagement in a civil war, like the Battle of Camlan.

Such total silence on the great events which were so fundamentally changing the whole story of Britain, and which must have been continually on men's lips as news of fresh disasters came from the troubled and despoiled east, is startling. True, the *Annals* were compiled in Wales where the last of the Britons felt relatively secure in their diminished and inaccessible lands, but the silence is nevertheless hard to understand. We have to accept that the monks who kept these records had resigned themselves to the fact that the Roman island was for ever gone, that the cause of the Britons and the Christian church were alike lost, except in their own mountains and beleaguered kingdoms. War could harm them no more, and ruin could not be inflicted on an already ruined province. Battles and the rumours of distant wars were of no interest to them in their quiet cloisters. It was enough to remember the one great triumph their people had won at Badon, and Camlan, the last sad battle of the civil war, in which the victor of Badon had perished, his hard won victory rendered fruitless.

For the rest, they were content to record church matters: the change in the celebration of Easter, the birth of St Brigid, the death of St Patrick and the passing of bishops. It was only when the English were converted to Christianity by Augustine that the *Annals* mention them, almost in passing. The entry for 595 tells us that Columcille died, King Dunaut died, and 'Augustine converted the English to Christ'.

Augustine's conversion of the English in Kent led to long argument between his followers and the native church of the Britons. When Augustine left Rome, the Pope had given him authority over all the bishops in Britain. This claim was stubbornly rejected by the local bishops and there were long and angry discussions between the two factions. We would give much for a contemporary British account of the dispute with Augustine, yet the *Annals* are again silent. This silence provides further evidence of the complete isolation of the compilers of the *Annals* and some justification for Augustine's charge that the Britons had lamentably failed in their Christian duty in keeping so aloof from the pagan English, and in making no attempt to lead them to the faith.

After the conversion of the English the entries continue for some years to record the quiet deaths of bishops. But in the year 613 is recorded 'The battle of Cair Legion: and there fell Selim the son of Cinam.' Here again we are in contact with the English. Aethilfrith, the pagan king of Northumbria, had succeeded to the kingdom in 593 and had attacked the northern frontiers of the Britons; since they were by now an independent people confined to the lands they still inhabit, we may call them the Welsh. The name of the great walled city of Deva, built by the Romans as a military centre, was forgotten. But the Britons dimly remembered that it had once been garrisoned by a legion, the Twentieth, which bore the proud nickname of the 'Victorious'. So they called the city 'Castra Legionis', the camp of the Legion. This is the *Cair Legion* of the *Annals*, the Chester of the English. Here Aethilfrith attacked an army of the Welsh led by Solon, son of their king Cunain. The pagan English were victorious, and the rout of the Welsh became a massacre, in which their prince fell. Worse, 1,250 monks accompanied the Welsh army, standing apart from the battle and praying for victory. When King Aethilfrith saw them, he grimly remarked that if they were using the force of prayer against him, then they were as much his adversaries as if they had been armed soldiers, and ordered them to be slaughtered. These were the terrible events that lie behind the terse entry in the *Annals*: *Gueith Cair Legion*, the Battle of Chester.

Aethilfrith died as violently as he had lived and was succeeded by Edwin whom he had previously banished. The *Annals* record for 617 *Etguin incipit regnare*. 'Edwin began to reign.' (The Britons always had difficulty with the *V* and *W* of other languages, and transcribed them as *gu*, hence '*Etguin*'.) King Edwin was later converted to Christianity and the *Annals* record his baptism in 626. During the seventh century, events in the English kingdom of Northumbria are noted fairly continually. Caedwalla or Cadwallon, King of the Britons on Northumbria's border, waged war against Edwin, finally slaying him in battle. Two entries record these events:

629 The siege of King Catguallaun in the island of Glannauc.
630 . . . the Battle of Meicaren, and there was killed Etguin and his two sons, but Catguallaun was the victor.

There followed further fighting. Caedwalla defeated Edwin's successor Osric, after the latter had besieged him in York. But Caedwalla was in turn killed by the new king of Northumbria, Oswald, at the Battle of Denisesburn. This engagement was remembered by the Britons as the Battle within the Wall—Catscaul. King Oswald, after a brief reign of nine years, was himself killed in a battle against the Mercians. These events too are recorded in the *Annals*:

> 631 The Battle of Cantscaul [*sic*] in which Catguollaan [*sic*] perished.
>
> 644 The Battle of Cocboy, in which there perished Oswald, king of the Nords, and Eoba, king of the Mercians.

It is evident that, for this period at least, the *Annals* were being kept somewhere to the north of the British territory, for events in the English kingdoms of Northumbria and Mercia continue to be recorded. 657 marks the death of 'Pantha' who is the pagan king Penda of Mercia. In 658 Osguid (King Oswiu of Northumbria) carried off plunder.

In 665 there is another tantalising entry: 'Easter was first celebrated among the Saxons. The second Battle of Badon.' Almost certainly it was fought between the Britons and their ancient enemies the English, on the same field as Arthur's still-remembered victory. We can imagine the army of the Britons looking with awe and apprehension at the hill where their ancestors had routed the invader 150 years before, and had brought a generation of peace to the beleaguered island. Here their strength was to be tested and their courage measured against the prowess of those ancestors, who had here conquered under their legendary leader Arthur. The record is silent, but it is tempting to believe that they were victorious, and that when the battle was over, with the English in retreat, they buried their dead, watched night gather in the sky, and dreamed for a while that they would one day repossess the proud cities and rich countryside that once had been theirs.

For the next hundred years there are hardly any entries on church matters, the births of saints or the deaths of bishops. Now it is the deaths of Saxon kings which are recorded, as if it was at last recognised that the island was Saxon, and that these were the only events of note. There is plague in 682, blood-coloured rain in 689, and a hot summer in 721. But it is the Saxon kings who now dominate the record.

In 760 there is war between the Britons and the English with a battle fought at 'Hirford', today's Hereford. Now the record is only concerned with the English as raiders and enemies. We are told of the deaths of local princes, of the devastation of the Welsh lands by Offa, King of Mercia, of the death of Caratauc, King of Gwynnedd, at the hands of the Saxons and of the death in 809 of Elbodg, his Archbishop. The records are now purely Welsh, and the acts of the English are noted only when they impinge upon the Welsh themselves. The English are seen as slayers of the Welsh kings, as devastators of the Welsh lands, but now the affairs of Wales are the chief matters recorded.

Although Manuscript A closes in 977, Manuscript B continues well beyond that date. The last two entries before 1066 are still entirely Welsh.

> 1063 Griffin, most noble son of Lewelin, King of the Britons, to their sorrow was killed
> Annus: Joseph, Bishop of Menevia, died.

In 1066, the Annals record that King Harold of Norway planned the conquest of England, but another Harold, Godwin's son, killed him in a sudden battle. But he, while still rejoicing over his victory, was deprived of his kingdom by William the Bastard, Duke of the Normans.

The *Annals* tell the sad history of the Britons' overthrow. Once heirs to Rome and rulers of all Britain, they became rulers only of that narrow and mountainous region which we call Wales. Here they slowly accepted their defeat and their isolation, but they never quite forgot the glories of their splendid past. Lewelin, the last king whose name is recorded in the *Annals*, is not described as king of a region but bears the proud title of *Rex Britonum*, king of the Britons, the scribe thus dismissing as usurpers the Saxon kings in the east, who were still seen as the barbarian rulers of an alien nation.

The *Annales Cambriae* form the basis of another document, entitled *Brut y Tywysogion* or the *Chronicle of the Princes of Wales*. This work is written in Welsh, and the most complete version is contained in the *Red Book of Hergest* at Jesus College, Oxford. This copy was made some time in the fourteenth century. The work has been ascribed to Caradoc of Llancarfan, the reputed author of the life of Gildas which we have already examined. If this be so, then the *Chronicle* must originally have been compiled about the middle of the twelfth century which was when Caradoc flourished. The *Chronicle* has all the appearance of belonging to a period as late as this.

Very little is known about Caradoc. According to Geoffrey of Monmouth, whose writings will be examined in Chapter IX, he was alive during the middle of the twelfth century. Geoffrey made him one of his literary heirs, in the sense that he bequeathed to Caradoc the task of continuing Geoffrey's own work and of writing a history of the Princes of Wales, largely because he knew the Welsh language. Geoffrey claimed that he gave to others the task of dealing with Saxon affairs, leaving it to Caradoc to continue the story of the Britons in their own land of Wales. The following is the passage from Geoffrey of Monmouth in which he names his successors:

> The princes who ruled afterwards in Wales I committed to Caradoc of Lancarfan, who was my contemporary, and to him I left the materials to write that book. The Saxon kings who succeeded consecutively I committed to William of Malmesbury and Henry of Huntingdon, and commended them to write concerning the Saxon kings, and omit the Welsh, as they are not possessed of that Welsh book which Walter archdeacon of Ox-

ford translated from the Latin, wherein he treats truly and fully of the above Welshmen: and I retranslated the whole from the Welsh into Latin.

This passage is to some extent borne out by the contents of the *Chronicle* itself. Geoffrey of Monmouth's work ends with the abdication of 'Cadwalla, King of the Britons', and his death at Rome as a sick old man. This is pure fiction. King Caedwalla of the Britons, as we have seen, died in battle at Denisesburn. Geoffrey is confusing him with Caedwalla, King of Wessex, who came to the throne in 685 and who (according to the *Anglo-Saxon Chronicle*) died in Rome, still a young man, three years later. Geoffrey has built a complicated and circumstantial structure of legend. After 'King Cadwalla of the Britons' died in Rome, says Geoffrey, 'the Britons embalmed his body, and encased it in a bronze statue which, mounted upon a bronze horse, was set up by the west gate of London as a monument to his victories and 'as a terror to the Saxons'. Geoffrey was not the first, and certainly not the last historian, to draw wrong conclusions from his sources. In such manner are legends born and too often they obstinately survive.

Whatever the rights and wrongs of Geoffrey's story, the *Chronicle of the Princes of Wales* opens in 681, the supposed year of the death of Kadwaladyr, which is the version of the name in this document. For the most part, the *Chronicle* is based firmly on the *Welsh Annals* from which it has a large measure been transcribed. New matter has occasionally been added—some historical, some legendary—and the entries of the *Annals* are frequently expanded. For instance, for the year 682 the *Annals* state briefly 'There was a great mortality in Britain in which Catgualart son of Catguolaum died.' The author of the *Chronicle*, mindful of Geoffrey's story, recognised the date as approximately right for the death of King Caedwalla, and seized on the name of Catgualart as being sufficiently similar to justify his identifying the one with the other. So three real personages are fused together: King Caedwalla of the Britons who died at

Denisesburn, King Caedwalla of Wessex who died in Rome, and Catgualart the son of Catgualaum who died of the plague in Wales! It is only rarely that we can see the separate strands of a myth so clearly and are able to recognise the several truths which together make up the fiction.

Against the year 681 (a discrepancy of one year) the *Chronicle of the Princes of Wales* accordingly records:

> It was the 681st year of Christ when the great mortality took place over the whole island of Britain. And from the beginning of the world until that time, it was one year less than 5880 years. And in that year Kadwaladyr the blessed, son of Kadwallawn, son of Catuan, King of the Britons, died at Rome on the 12th May; as Vyrdin had formerly prophesied to Wrtheyrn [Vortigern] of the foul lips. And thenceforth the Britons lost the crown of the kingdom and the Saxons gained it.

The death in Britain of Catgualart during the plague, as recorded in the *Annals*, has now become the death of Kadwaladyr, King of the Britons, at Rome. Even a precise day of the month is given for the non-existent event! The author has, moreover, turned to legends already ancient to fill out his story. Vyrdin is of course Myrddin—the Merlin of the fables. And here we have a prophecy of his (made to Vortigern and therefore dating to about 450) fulfilled 230 years later.

The *Chronicle* then records that King Cadwalader the Blessed was succeeded by Ivor of Armorica (Brittany) who reigned for forty-eight years, not as a king but as a chief or prince.

For some 200 years the *Chronicle of the Princes of Wales* is little more than a translation of the *Welsh Annals*. It follows Manuscript B very closely, which again suggests a fairly late date for its compilation and is consistent with Caradoc's authorship of the work. From the late 900s onwards—that is to say after the main version of the *Annals* had ended—there are indications that the author of the *Chronicle* had some additional sources of information. For example under 951 the *Chronicle* shows the deaths of two sons of Howel, yet the *Annals* record the death of Rotri, son of Higuel, in 954. For 952, the *Chronicle* entry is again much fuller. The *Annals* report briefly that there was great slaughter between the sons of Idwal and the sons of Hoeli in the place that is called Gurguist. Anarant the son of Guiriat was killed. Guin the son of Hoeli died. The *Chronicle* tells in addition of two leaders, sons of Wryat, killed by the pagans. It adds that Keredigyawn (Ceredigion) was devastated by the sons of Idwal and that Etwin (Edwin), the son of Howel the Good, died. Edwin seems to be the 'Guin' of the *Annals*. The *Chronicle* seems to be have used a different and fuller source. Similarly, the bare entry in the *Annals* of the death in 975 of the English King Edgar appears in the *Chronicle* as 974, with the added information that Dunwallaon, King of Strathclyde, went to Rome.

Typical of these fuller entries is the account of the war waged by the Welsh against 'Rein the Scot'. In the *Annals* it is dated 1022. We are briefly told that 'Reyn the Scot', who falsely claimed to be the son of Maredut, a British king, was attacked and killed by King Seisil of Venedotia (Gwynnedd). Eilef (possibly Olaf the Danish leader) devastated Demetia, and Menevia was destroyed. The *Chronicle* for the year 1020 tells a much fuller story. Rein the Scot was accepted by the Britons in the south and proclaimed king. Llywelyn made war against him. (Llywelyn, the son of Seisyll, is described as supreme king of Gwynedd; his kingdom was immensely rich and extended from sea to sea. There were no poor men or deserted villages in his lands.) Rein advanced proudly and with great show, 'as is the manner of the Scots', confident of victory. But the men of Gwynnedd stood firm and Rein, brave in attack, beat a cowardly retreat. Llywelyn's army pursued the defeated host to the borders of Mercia, killing many and laying waste the countryside. We are not told, as in the *Annals*, that Rein was slain, but simply that he was never seen again. Then the devastation of Dyved and the destruction of Menevia are briefly described.

The *Chronicle* entry for 1066 is again somewhat fuller than that of the *Annals*. We are told that King Harold of Norway (who has now become 'Heralt of Denmark'!) contemplated the conquest of the Saxons. But the other Harold, son of Godwin, attacked and slew him. No credit is given to the English army for their defeat of the men of Norway at Stamford Bridge. They had force-marched north and, weary from their long summer journey, they had attacked. The battle was long and stubborn but at last the Norwegians gave way. To the Welsh chronicler the victory was not due to the courage and resolution of the English; they won by making a surprise attack while their enemies were unarmed, and were 'aided by national treachery'. Harold of England is seen as a usurper, who had taken the crown after the death of Edward the Confessor 'through cruelty'. His defeat by William of Normandy was seen as fitting retribution. 'And that William defended the kingdom of England with an invincible hand and his most noble army.' The descendants of the vanquished Britons were not sorry to see the triumphant Saxons conquered in their turn. Their joy was short-lived, for the Normans later attacked Wales.

These two Welsh documents have taken us through the last chapters of the story of the Britons. Gildas told us of the first British defeats, and their great recovery at Badon. There was still cause for exhortation, in his day, if not for hope. Some return to the old virtues might yet have been possible. But in the *Welsh Annals* and the *Chronicle of the Princes of Wales*, we see the Britons gradually accepting their fate. No longer the heirs of the island, bereft alike of hope and the means to inflict any final defeat upon the Saxons, they now dwelt in the narrow confines of Wales, defending their frontiers. Sometimes they taught a bloody lesson to the arrogant Saxons on their borders, but for the most part they fought one another in a series of civil wars that woefully echoed Gildas's angry lament. Yet through all their defeat and decline two things remained: pride in their past and hatred for the Saxon.

III

NENNIUS—THE HISTORY OF THE BRITONS

THE last document to give an account of the Saxon conquest of Britain from the British point of view is a short book written in Latin and called *Historia Britonum* (*The History of the Britons*). It seems to embody at least some material contemporary with the earliest events it describes.

Unlike both the *Welsh Annals* and the *Chronicle of the Princes of Wales*, it not a simple year-by-year account of events as they took place, maintained from generation to generation. It is a largely successful attempt to write a coherent history of the past. Events are described in much more detail and greater depth, so that a far fuller picture is given of what was happening in the island during the dark, savage years of the Anglo-Saxon conquest. It enables us to see the period as a whole and follow the broad sweep of events, rather than catching mere glimpses of disjointed episodes. On the other hand the firm framework of dates within which the compilers of the *Annals* were working disciplined their writing into an orderliness and clarity which the *History* sometimes lacks. However unreliable and imprecise the dating in the *Annals* may be, at least we know that the events have been recorded in chronological order, and we have an approximate idea of when they occurred. *The History of the Britons* gives very few dates in the earlier sections, so that there are hardly any fixed landmarks to enable a path to be mapped through the formless and shadowy landscape.

Because of the enormous reputation enjoyed by Gildas, it was believed for many years that he was the author of the *History*. The later chroniclers, William of Malmesbury, Henry of Huntingdon and Geoffrey of Monmouth, all ascribe the *History* to him. The Norman poet Geffrei of Gaimar, who wrote a rhymed history of the English nation towards the middle of the twelfth century, refers to Arthur, reporting that he fought the 'Danes' and attracted much hatred by slaying many men in his battles against 'Modret', whom he later killed.

Et les nevoz Artur regnerent,
Ki encontre Engleis guereierent.
Meis li Daneis mult haient,
Pur lur parenz, ki morz estaient
Es batailles ke Artur fist
Contre Modret, k'il puis oscist.

Now although Gildas does not mention Arthur by name, Geffrei goes on to say that all this has been recounted by Gildas:

Si co est veir ke Gilde dist,
En la geste, trova escrit.

The History of the Britons does, in fact, mention Arthur. Moreover, since Geffrei is referring to Arthur's battle against Mordred, recorded in the *Welsh Annals*, it seems that this work too was thought to have been written by Gildas the Wise.

The *History* appears to have been immensely popular, and there are about thirty manuscript copies in existence. Five of these, made in the thirteenth and fourteenth centuries, are prefaced by a short prologue said to have been written by Nennius, described as a student of St Elbod. It is entitled 'The Apologia of Nennius, Historian of the British People' and reads:

> I Nennius, a student of St Elbod, have taken care to write down a few extracts which the carelessness of the people of Britain had cast aside, because teachers here had no skill, nor did they set down any records in their books about this island of Britain. But I have collected together all that I have found, both from the histories of the Romans as well as from the chronicles of the church Fathers (Hieronymus, Eusebuis, Isidorus, Prosperus), and also from the writings of the Scots and the English and from the traditions of our old men. Many teachers and writers have tried to write this but have given up the task because of I know not what difficulties, and because of frequent epidemics and numerous wars. I ask every reader who shall read this book to give me pardon for having written these things down after so many have failed—like a chattering bird or some unqualified judge! I am willing to give place to any man who knows more about these skills than I do.

St Elbod, whose name is given in at least one of the manuscripts as Elvodugus, may well be the Bishop Elbodogus who is twice mentioned in the *Welsh Annals*. The first reference to him occurs in 768 when, we are told, the Britons changed their method of dating Easter, the reform having been introduced by 'Elbodugus, a man of God'. The second is against the year 809 and reads: 'Elbodg, Archbishop of the kingdom of Gwynedd departed to God.' If Nennius had been a pupil of this Archbishop, then we have some evidence for the period when he worked. There is another and more precise clue to his dates. One of the manuscript copies (written towards the end of the twelfth or beginning of the thirteenth century) contains not only the prologue already quoted but also a longer version. In this, Nennius repeats that he had been a pupil of Elbod. He adds:

> Therefore this work, written in order to help my inferiors and not through envy of my superiors, was written in the year 858 of our Lord's incarnation.

Given that Nennius entered his monastery as a boy and that he was a pupil of Elbod towards the end of the latter's life, the

Page 67: Page from the copy of the *Annales Cambriae* made on the flyleaves of an abridged copy of *Domesday Book*. Key, page 202.

iafeth alan' cum trib; filiis suis. quorũ nomina
sunt. hessitio. armeno. negue. hissitio autem ha
buit filios quattuor. hi sunt francus. roman'. brit
to alban'. Armenon autẽ habuit quinq; filios.
goth'. ualagoth'. gebid'. burgand'. langobardus.
N eugo autẽ habuit autẽ tres filios. uandal'. saxo.
boguar'.

Ab hisitione autẽ. Orte sunt quattuor gen
tes. franci. latini. albani. & britti. Ab armi
none autẽ quinque. gothi. ualagothi. gebidi.
burgandi. langobardi. A neguio uero quattuor.
boguarii. uandali. Saxones. & taringi. Iste au
tẽ gentes sub diuise sunt p tota europã. Alan'.
autem ut aiunt. fili' fuit fetebir. filii ougomun.
filii thoi. filii boib. filii simeon. filii mair. filii aur
thach. filii oth. filii abir. filii ra. filii ezra. filii iz
rau. filii baath. filii iobaath. filii iouan. filii ia
feth. filii noe. filii lamech. filii matusalẽ. filii
enoch. filii iareth. filii malaleel. filii cainan.
filii enos. filii seth. filii adam. filii dĩ uiui. hanc
peritiã inueni ex traditione ueterũ. qui inco
le inprimo fuer' brittannię.

Brittones a bruto. brut' fili' hisitionis. hisiti
on alanei. alaneus fili' reae. filię siluię
reae. filię numę pampilii. filii ascanii. ascani'
fili' enee. filii anchise. filii troi. filii darda
ni. filii flise. filii iuuani. filii iafeth. Iafeth
uero habuit septẽ filios. prim' gomer. a quo me
dos. Quart' iuuan a quo greci. Quint' tubal.
a quo ebrei & hispani & itali. Sext' mosoch.
a quo cappadoces. Septimus tiras a quo traces.
hi sunt filii iafeth. filii noe. filii lamech.

Et redeam nunc ad id de quo digressus sũ.

Romani autẽ dũ acciperent dominiu
totius mundi. ad brittannos miserunt
legatos ut obsides & censũ acciperent ab
illis. Sic accipiebant ab uniuersis regionib;
& insulis. Brittanni autẽ cũ essent tiranni
& tumidi. legationẽ romanoꝝ contẽpser'.

Page 68: Page from a late tenth-or early eleventh-century manuscript of the works of Nennius. Key, page 204.

book could have been the crowning achievement of a lifetime of study. Nennius might then have been in his early sixties. We may therefore take 858 as a likely date for the work.

The claim made in the prologue that the book is based upon older written material as well as old traditions is borne out by the work itself. It has been argued that those chapters which deal in great detail with the coming of the Saxons under Hengist during the reign of Vortigern have probably been taken from a lost Romano-British account written only a few years after the events described, and that later chapters dealing with events in the north of England were based on a contemporary English chronicle completed about 685—the date of the collapse of the kingdom of Northumbria. Certainly, the narrative of these events ends abruptly at that time. Had this section of the *History* been written by a Briton, a mere observer of events in Northumbria, there appears to be no reason why the account should have ended then, for there were many British events to record after 685. But if this section was taken from a lost Northumbrian chronicle, then there was every reason for the latter to have ceased when the kingdom fell. Where a British chronicler would have rejoiced, a Northumbrian scribe would have mourned; sorrow and the ruin of defeat would have silenced him.

The *History* opens by dividing mankind's past into six ages, based upon biblical events. The first is from Adam to the Flood, and the sixth is from the time of John the Baptist to the Day of Judgement. This method does not lend itself to very precise dating, as we, of course, live in the same age as Nennius!

We are told that the island of Britain takes its name from Brutus, a Roman Consul. There follows a geographical description, much of which is taken directly from the opening chapter of Gildas. The island is 800 miles long and 200 miles wide. It contained twenty-eight cities (the number varies in some manuscripts). The names of all of these are given in the language of the Britons. Each name is prefixed with the word *Cair* (a late form of the Latin *castra*, a camp or garrison). York is *Cair Ebrauc*,

Gloucester is *Cair Glovi*, London is *Cair Londein* and so on.

The three main islands are listed, the Isle of Wight, the Isle of Man and the Orkneys. There are many rivers but, as with Gildas, only two are named—Thames and Severn. Along these, in former days, many ships came bringing wealth and trade. (In this passage we have Nennius the editor, not Nennius the writer. The phrase is taken directly from Gildas. By the middle of the ninth century when Nennius was writing, communications with the Continent were once more well established and London was again, as it had been in Roman times, a busy commercial centre. Nennius himself would hardly have used such a nostalgic phrase about the trade and traffic of former days. Gildas on the other hand was looking back with sorrow to the busy days of Roman Britain, the memory of which had not yet altogether faded. The fact that here, where we can recognise Nennius's source, he repeats a passage which was no longer historically or emotionally relevant entitles us to believe that many other sections of his book are fairly faithful extracts from older documents, the originals of which are now lost.)

Nennius next examines how Britain was first populated. He tells us that there were two separate versions. According to the first, the island was peopled by the descendants of Silvius Posthumus, a son of Aeneas and Lavinia, born after his father's death. The island was later subdued by Brutus, Consul of Rome. The inhabitants took the name of Britons after their conqueror. The second story is that after Aeneas became king of the Romans, his wife Lavinia had a son named Silvius. Ascanius, an elder son of Aeneas, married and his wife became pregnant. She was examined by a soothsayer who announced that the child would be a son. He would be the bravest of all the Italians, and beloved of all men. Ascanius put the soothsayer to death. The child (whose mother died in giving birth to him) was named Brutus. While still a boy, he accidentally slew his father with an arrow and was banished. He travelled into Gaul and at length came to this island where he settled and the land was peopled by his descendants. It became known as 'Britannia', taking its name from Brutus.

Both these are clearly fable. It is disappointing that Nennius did not reveal his sources. Perhaps the tales are a tradition of the Britons dating from the time of the Roman occupation, when all things Roman were esteemed, and not to be Roman was to be barbarous.

It has been suggested that the legend of being descended from Aeneas of the royal house of Troy arose from the name of one of the tribes in the south-east of Britain, the Trinovantes, who were mentioned by Caesar. He described them as probably the most powerful tribe in that region. They were among the first to seek the protection of Rome. One of their princes, Mandubracius, fled from his enemies to join Caesar on the Continent before the Roman invasion. Once the Romans were installed in Britain, and Roman history and myth had become part of the folklore of the Britons, it needed little imagination (and less scholarship!) to interpret Trinovantes as a corruption of *Troii novantes*, the new Trojans. It was a legend that must have nourished the self-esteem of the Britons during the prosperous years of the Roman occupation, identifying them as it did with the Greco-Roman world, source of all things civilised. The proud belief has persisted that the inhabitants of this island are descended from the tragic royal house of Troy, whose towered city was sacked in a night of blood and flames by Agamemnon's triumphant army. London was referred to as New Troy, and belief in the legend is not quite dead even today.

Nennius tells us how the Picts occupied the Orkney Islands, making them a base from which they made their forays to the mainland. They seized all the northern extremities of Britain where, says Nennius, they still retained possession of a third of the island.

Many years later the Scots came to Ireland from Spain. Again Nennius gives two alternative legends describing their arrival. In the first, a man called Partholomus (or Bartholomaeus) came with

1,000 men and women from Spain, and settled in Ireland. In time the population increased fourfold, but then a plague broke out and within a week all were dead. They were followed by a man named Nimech who, after a disastrous journey, made landfall in Ireland and stayed there for several years before returning again to Spain with all his people. Then set out three sons of a Spanish soldier, with thirty ships each containing thirty men and thirty women. (To the Britons, the number three was magical. It recurs in their legends as well as in early Welsh poetry.) They came across a great tower of glass on an island, and all the ships save one were lost when they attacked it. The thirty men and thirty women in the surviving ship landed on the island. It sank into the sea and they too were drowned. Finally, a man named Hoctor came from Spain, and his descendants were the Irish. Nennius seems here to be recording genuine folklore. The belief that Ireland was peopled by folk from Spain is very old and may well contain, behind the marvels and fables, genuine truth.

The second legend is that when Pharaoh's hosts rode in pursuit of the children of Israel, only to be stopped by the miracle of the Red Sea, there was a Scythian noble serving in the Egyptian army who would not ride with them against the Israelites. He was exiled from Egypt and, after many years of wandering, came at length with his family to Spain. One thousand and two years after the flight from Egypt, his descendants settled in Ireland. This legend, with its biblical basis, is obviously less ancient than the first, and probably represents an adaptation by Christians of some earlier story.

Nennius adds that the Britons came to Britain in the third age of mankind and the Scots came to Ireland in the fourth. The Britons were forever being attacked by the Picts from the north and the Scots from the west.

Then follow two brief chapters. One records that the first man to live in Europe was named Alanus and his descent is traced to Japhet. As his grandsons had such names as Francus,

Romanus, Gothus, Brutus, Burgundus and Saxo, each of whom fathered one of the nations of Europe, we need not take this section too seriously! The second chapter returns to the theme of Brutus, and traces his descent from Japhet. This, placed as it is out of logical order, could well be an insertion by a later copyist whose piety moved him to link the pagan legend of Aeneas with one of the Bible stories.

The rest of the book deals with firm historical events and we are able, at least in part, to check Nennius's account against reliable sources. From these tests Nennius sometimes emerges with credit—but not always.

The historical section opens soberly enough with the story of Julius Caesar's invasions of Britain. The accuracy of the narrative is somewhat marred by Nennius's preoccupation with the magic number three. He tells us that Caesar first came with sixty ships (*three* score), and fought unsuccessfully against King Belinus. *Three* years later he returned with *three* hundred ships but was again defeated. So he came again on a *third* expedition and finally defeated the Britons at Trinovantum in 47 BC. It is evident, in spite of the claim in the prologue that he consulted Roman historians, that Nennius had not referred to Caesar's own commentaries, in which he would have read that there were only two expeditions, in successive years, and from which the magic figure three is lamentably absent. In a sense, however, Nennius's account tells more than a direct copying of Caesar's own story would have done. It shows how the Britons retained their traditional memories of the Roman period, written in their own characteristic fashion. And it shows how we are entitled only to extract the barest truth from the decorated narratives of legend. From this tale, even if all other records had been lost, we could at least learn that Julius Caesar attacked Britain more than once, lost a number of ships and achieved no lasting success.

The story of the rest of the Roman period is told in a similar manner. There is a brief but good account of the conquest by Claudius, and of the death of Severus in York. The usurpation of power in Britain by Carausius is recorded, though his motives have been glamorised. Nennius records that his tomb was still to be seen. Strangely, nothing is said of Constantine the Great except that he was the son of Constantius. There is a very full account of Magnus Maximus, the Spanish officer who took the legions out of Britain, conquered Rome, and for a brief while ruled as Emperor before retribution overtook him at the Battle of Aquileia where he was defeated and slain.

Nennius then tells us of the troubled times in Britain now that the legions had vanished. Three times the Romans sent deputies to Britain, to re-establish Rome's rule. All these the Britons put to death. (Again the magic number three makes it evident that this tale is not true as it stands.) Some attempt may have been made by Rome to bring Britain back into the Empire, and this attempt may well have been rebuffed.

The Britons in their turn, because of attacks by the Picts and Scots, sent a humble delegation to Rome, seeking help. The account of this mission closely resembles that of Gildas from whom Nennius has no doubt taken it. Help was sent, as Gildas has already told us, and this passage probably refers to the victorious expeditionary force which came to Britain under Stilicho in about 395.

The next seventeen chapters deal in detail with the reign of King Guorthigirnus (King Vortigern, whom we have already met). They recount the coming of the Saxons into Britain under Hengist, and their long struggle with the Britons. This section appears to be a complete document in itself, beginning with the coming of the Saxons and ending with the death of the two leaders, Vortigern and Hengist. There is internal evidence to suggest that the account was originally written very soon after the events described, and that Nennius was merely transcribing an old Romano-British document.

The section opens somewhat abruptly with the bald statement 'Vortigern then reigned in Britain'. The Britons were in terror of the Romans, and of incursions by the Picts and Scots.

There were fears, too, about Ambrosius, a leader in today's Devon and Cornwall. This passage suggests that there was rivalry, if not hostility, between Ambrosius and Vortigern.

In the meantime three ships came bringing exiles from Germany. Their leaders were Hengist and Horsa, two brothers who traced their descent back to the god Godwolf. Vortigern received them as friends and gave them the Isle of Thanet. This was in 447, says Nennius, a date which agrees closely with Gildas's independent account, which records that the Britons made their last desperate appeal to Rome in 446. Allowing time for the message to reach Rome and for the reply, 447 seems absolutely right for the arrival of the Saxons. This accord between the dates is all the more remarkable because Nennius here owes nothing to Gildas, but was working from a different and independent source. Unlike Gildas (and this demonstrates the independence of his material) Nennius does not state that Vortigern invited the Saxons to Britain, but simply that he came to an arrangement with them once they had arrived. His dating bears the ring of truth.

After the Saxons had spent some time on Thanet, Vortigern promised them clothing and supplies on condition that they would help in the defence of Britain. He could not fulfil his promise because of the large number of settlers, and when Hengist did not get the supplies, he sent to the Continent for reinforcements. Sixteen ships arrived bearing amongst others Hengist's own daughter.

Hengist invited Vortigern to a feast where the wine and mead flowed freely. Vortigern fell in love with Hengist's daughter. Hengist, having consulted his elders (Nennius tells us that they were of the 'Oghgul' race, which may be a corrupt form of 'Angle') consented to his daughter's marriage to Vortigern. In return for his consent, Vortigern gave his new father-in-law the kingdom of Kent, without telling the local king.

Hengist then persuaded Vortigern to allow him to bring over his son and brother, suggesting that they should be settled in the north, near Hadrian's Wall. The number of settlers thus continued to grow.

Meanwhile, Vortigern married his own daughter, by whom he had a son. This tale is the less difficult to believe when we remember the eloquent charges made by Gildas against the various British kings. Incest appears to have been fairly common amongst them, and indeed was almost an occupational hazard. Vortigern was rebuked for his sin, and his council of twelve wise men advised him to withdraw to the boundaries of his kingdom and there build a fortified city for his better defence.

He came to Gwynnedd and selected an impregnable site for his citadel on the top of a high mountain. Building began, but one night all the work vanished. The council advised him that he would not succeed in building the citadel until he had found a child born without a father, whom he should kill and with whose blood he should sprinkle the ground. Such a boy was found and brought to the king, who explained his purpose. The boy then told the king that under the pavement where they stood there was a pool. The pavement was dug up and the pool discovered. The boy said that there were two vases in the pool, and this too proved true. In the vases, said the boy, there was a tent. They were opened and the tent was found. The boy then said that in the tent were two dragons, one white and one red. The tent was unfolded and the two dragons were seen. They began to fight. The white dragon threw down the other and drove him away. This was thrice repeated. At length the red dragon, although the weaker, drove the white dragon from the tent, chasing him through the pool until he disappeared. The boy then explained the omen. The pool represented the world. The white dragon represented the invaders from Germany and the red dragon represented the Britons—as indeed it does to this day. The omen showed that the red dragon of the Britons would ultimately drive the Saxons out of the island.

Although this tale is cast in the mould of legend rather than history, it is one of the most important passages in the section, helping us to assess the date and authenticity of the whole narrative. By 600 the Anglo-Saxons' grip on the country was secure and no one composing a document at that time or later could have prophesied the Saxons' final overthrow. This, then, must be an account of events written down some time in the sixth or very early seventh century. At such a date, the prophecy would have been not merely a heart-stirring trumpet call to the beleaguered but still resolute Britons, urging them to continue their obstinate struggle, it would also have been believed. At any significantly later date it would not.

The narrative continues with the boy telling Vortigern that his name is Ambrosius (in British *Embries Guletic.*) The last word, and its alternative form *Wledig*, is a British word meaning prince; while *Embries* (modern Welsh *Emrys*) is Ambrosius. Vortigern assigns his new city to the boy together with all the western provinces of Britain. This suggests that, for a time at least, Ambrosius held his western kingdom of Devon and Cornwall under the suzerainty of Vortigern.

Vortigern's son Vortimer then fought Hengist's men, driving them back to the Isle of Thanet, where he penned them in. But the invaders sent ships across the grey North Sea to their friends in Germany, who sent over huge numbers of strong and warlike men. Hostilities were resumed, in the course of which first one side and then the other was victorious. Vortimer fought four pitched battles against the invaders. (That the number of battles is given as four, and not the conventional three, suggests that this may be true.) Vortimer died, having first enjoined his soldiers to bury him at the entrance to the place where the Saxons had first landed, as this would ensure that the invaders would never remain in the island. His wishes were ignored with the results we know.

After this, the Saxons became firmly established. Vortigern remained their friend because of his love for Hengist's daughter to whom he was still married—although he had other wives too.

After Vortimer's death, Hengist fatally weakened the Britons' cause by a terrible act of treachery. He invited Vortigern, with 300 of his nobles and officers, to a feast. There, at a prearranged signal given by Hengist, they were all stabbed by Hengist's men as they sat at table, Saxon hosts and British guests side by side. Vortigern himself escaped.

A brief paragraph follows which appears to be a confused folk-memory of the visit paid to Britain by St Germanus some twenty or thirty years before. We are told, quite anachronistically, that the saint was appointed as the commander of the army of the Britons. St Germanus, the soldier-bishop who came from Gaul in 428 to help the Britons in their spiritual as well as military difficulties, won a great battle against a combined force of Picts and Saxons. This battle is known as the Alleluia Victory, since Alleluia was used by St Germanus both as a signal and as a battle cry. A memory of this battle appears to have prompted Nennius to record that, some thirty years later, Germanus defeated the Saxons 'not by the clamour of trumpets, but by praying and singing Alleluia', and by his army's cries to God. King Vortigern then perished in a fire with Hengist's daughter and his other wives.

The section ends with a list of the sons of Vortigern and a genealogy going back some seventeen generations. The presence of the genealogy again strongly suggests that the whole section is based on a single self-contained document giving a detailed account of Vortigern's reign, and ending appropriately with his long and royal lineage. Seventeen generations take us back about 500 years, which means that his ancestors may have been kings of some region of Britain in Caesar's day. That his family was Christian is indicated by the names on the genealogy. There is one Theodore among them (*Theudubr*) and more than one Paul.

Was Vortigern as evil as the portrait Gildas painted of him? Was he indeed 'Vortigern of the foul lips' as the *Welsh Annals* say? Gildas, writing 100 years after the struggle with Hengist, knowing the outcome and full of bitterness at the tragic collapse of his people, saw Vortigern as a besotted villain and a fool. The picture drawn by Nennius, apparently based upon a contemporary record, is certainly more sympathetic. We see him as a man beset by powerful enemies, with no fleet to prevent the landing of squadron after squadron of the curved and dragon-prowed ships from Germany, endeavouring to maintain his kingdom, trying to make obedient allies (as the wise Romans had done) of the warlike barbarians. He was threatened by armies immensely stronger and more ruthless than his own, and the victim of terrible treachery when hundreds of his high officers and nobles were butchered by the merciless Saxons. Nennius does not merely supplement the record; he adds a depth of truth to the flat drawing of Gildas—a drawing that comes dangerously close to caricature.

At the end of this account of Vortigern's reign (of which Nennius was the editor rather than the author) there follows a brief history of St Patrick, adding little to the main narrative; like the account of St Germanus, it was probably added by some pious hand. A brief new section now begins, and appears to be based upon a lost document of the sixth or early seventh century. 'At that time', the first three words, suggest that it is an extract. Nennius does not define the time to which he referred. It is as though he had omitted a paragraph in which notable events were recorded that would have given meaning to the opening phrase.

> At that time, the Saxons increased in strength and grew in numbers throughout Britain.

The account goes on to say that when Hengist died, his son left the northern part of Britain and returned to Kent. There follows the fascinating detail:

> Arthur was fighting against them in those days, with all the kings of Britain. But he himself was the general of the wars (*Dux bellorum*) and in all the wars he was the victor.

There is a marginal note in one of the manuscripts explaining that Arthur means 'The Dreadful Bear' or 'The Iron Hammer'. An alternative name is given, *Mab Uter*, which is said to mean in the tongue of the Britons 'The Dreadful Son', 'because from his boyhood he was bloodthirsty'. Arthur, as we know, died in a civil war, so that he had enemies among his fellow countrymen as well as among the Saxons. This reference to his cruelty seems to be an echo of what those enemies said to him. It helps us to see him as he was in the flesh; not the fairy-tale figure of romance, but a dedicated and ruthless soldier whose passionate qualities were seen as prowess by his friends and as cruelty by his detractors.

Nennius then lists in detail the twelve battles in which Arthur led the Britons to victory, and gives the ancient British names of where they were fought. These have faded from our maps so that none can now be firmly identified. He writes that in one of these battles Arthur carried an image of the Virgin Mary upon his shoulders; he put the pagans to flight, and many died. Arthur, then, was a Christian, using a Christian standard and defending a Christian civilisation against the still-pagan Saxons.

In one of the manuscripts there is a note that Arthur once visited Jerusalem and had had a cross made there of the same dimensions as the True Cross. For three days he fasted and watched, praying that the Lord would give him victory 'through this sign' over the pagans. The annotator here confuses Arthur with the Emperor Constantine who saw in the sky a great cross of light, and an angel told him to make this his ensign and 'in this sign conquer!' This is pure myth and is in marked contrast with the narrative itself.

The twelfth battle listed is 'the Battle of Mount Badon in which there fell, in one day, 840 men in one charge of Arthur; and no one slew them but he himself alone'.

This last phrase has caused many to assume that Nennius was describing a mere fairyland adventure, with the great Arthur improbably slaying hundreds of his enemies with his own sword.

But surely the phrase must be taken together with the earlier words that he was fighting 'with all the kings of Britain'. The point being made is that at Badon he was fighting without these kings and that it was his army, and his alone, that inflicted a great defeat upon the Saxons.

This is all that we are told about Arthur. And the extract from the lost chronicle, if such it be, is tantalisingly brief. It is obviously drawn from another, fuller source than either Gildas or the *Welsh Annals*, and therefore independently confirms that the victor of Mount Badon was the now legendary Arthur. It is also interesting that in this, the first detailed reference to the hero, he is not called a king. Indeed, in contrast to the kings of Britain who fought by his side, he is definitely said to have been the *dux bellorum*, or commander-in-chief.

Having told the story of Arthur, the *History* now turns to Saxon matters and gives the genealogies of the kings of the various Anglo-Saxon kingdoms. Then there are entries dealing with events in the North, on the troubled frontier lands where Saxon Northumbria confronted the lands of the Britons. This section appears to be based on a Northumbrian source, possibly a list of kings. In 547, King Ida ruled over Northumbria. After twelve years he died and was succeeded by Gluppa who reigned for a year. Then came Adda, who was succeeded by Aethelric. There followed Theodric and Erithuwald and Hussa. Nennius records all this very accurately, adding details from the British side:

> Ida the son of Eobba held regions in the area north of the Humber for twelve years and joined together Dinguerin and Guirbirneth. Then Dutigern at that time fought stoutly against the nation of the English. Then Talhaern Tataguen was famous for his poetry, and Neirin [Aneurin] and Taliessin and Bluchbard . . . at one and the same time were famous for their poetry.
>
> Mailcun the great king was ruling among the Britons, in the region of Guenodota [Gwynned] . . .
>
> Adda son of Ida reigned eight years. Adlric son of Aethbric

> son of Adda reigned four years. Deoric [Theodric] son of Ida reigned seven years. Friodolguald [Frithuwald] reigned six years, in whose time the kingdom of Kent received baptism from a mission sent by Gregory. Hussa reigned seven years. Four kings fought against him, Urbgen and Riderch-hen and Gwallanc and Morcant.
>
> Deoric fought powerfully against the same Urbgen with his sons. . . And Urbgen beset them in the island of Metcaud [Lindisfarne] for three days. And while he was on this expedition he was slaughtered at the instigation of Morcant through envy because in him, more than in all other kings, there was the greatest prowess in waging war.

The accuracy with which Nennius records the names of the kings of Northumbria suggests that when he had a good source he used it well. His account of the fierce resistance still being offered by the Britons in the north can be given credence. That Urbgen could besiege the Northumbrian leaders on Lindisfarne means that the avenging armies of the Britons had swept across the whole width of Northumbria, driving the desperate English to the coast. The account is a reminder of how stubbornly and long the Britons fought back and how, more than once, they had defeated their powerful enemies.

Urbgen is of course the 'Sir Urien' of the romances, in which he is described as Arthur's brother-in-law and father of Ywaine. He is mentioned in the poems of Taliessin and was evidently a great hero. Unfortunately Nennius's account is confused. If Urbgen had been slain by Morcant in the reign of Theodric (who died in 579) he could not have fought against Hussa, who began to reign in 585. Given, however, that he was leading his armies against either of these kings, history here comes to the support of legend. As we have seen in the *Welsh Annals*, Arthur died in 570. It is certainly possible that Urbgen could have been alive ten or fifteen years later, bravely continuing the struggle which Arthur had so gallantly led. Then, just as Arthur had died in civil war at the hands of Mordred, so Urbgen died at the hands of his own people. The disunity of the Britons, of which Gildas wrote so bitterly, seems to have persisted and to have undone all that was gained by such dramatic victories as Badon and Lindisfarne.

In 626 King Edwin of Northumbria was converted to Christianity and baptised in York, where he appointed Paulinus as Archbishop. Nennius adds: 'If anyone wishes to know who baptised these people, Ruin the son of Urbgen baptised them.' It is generally held that Paulinus baptised the King, but perhaps the son of the heroic Urbgen was at least present at the ceremony. It is tempting to believe that the great nephew of Arthur was still continuing the defence of the Christian cause, not by the sword but through the faith itself.

Edwin's conversion did not stop him fighting the Christian Britons. He occupied Elmet, a kingdom of the Britons that lay in the West Riding of Yorkshire, the name of which still survives in village names. We are then told of his death at the Battle of Meicen at the hands of Cadwallon, King of the Britons in Gwynnedd. The death of Cadwallon at the hands of Oswald of Northumbria is also recorded:

> and Oswald himself killed Catgublaun [Cadwallon] King of Guenedota [Gwynned] in the Battle of Catscaul.

This is the Battle of Denisesburn, and Nennius's word is a corruption of Catisgual, 'The Battle within the Wall'.

This Northumbrian section ends with the death of Penda, the heathen King of Mercia:

> Penda the son of Pybba reigned ten years. He himself first separated the Kingdom of Mercia from the Kingdom of Northumbria, and slew Onna King of the East Angles, and Oswald King of the Northmen by treachery. He fought the battle of Cocboy in which there fell Eoua the son of Pippa his brother, King of the Mercians, and Oswald King of the Northumbrians, and himself was victor through the art of the devil. He was not baptised and he never believed in God.

King Penda had fought side by side with the great Cadwallon and had laid waste the whole of Northumbria. The Britons must have seen him as a brave war leader with whose help they might annihilate the English kingdom of Northumbria. But Nennius's account of Penda is hostile, and here he seems to be still using a Northumbrian document in which such hostility would be natural. The Battle of Cocboy is called the Battle of Winwidfeld in the *Anglo-Saxon Chronicle* and is recorded as having taken place in 654.

The *History* of Nennius falls into several clearly defined parts:

1 A geographical description of Britain largely drawn from Gildas.
2 The legendary origins of the Britons, the Picts and the Scots, almost certainly derived from Romano-British traditions.
3 An account of the Roman period, drawn partly from good classical sources and partly (as in the case of Julius Caesar's invasions) from folk memory.
4 A legendary life of St Germanus.
5 An account of Vortigern's reign, probably edited from a contemporary history now lost.
6 An account of Arthur's battles which may be an extract from a lost chronicle of Arthur written at the time of the events described.
7 An account of events in the north of England edited from a seventh-century Northumbrian document.

At the end of some of the manuscripts of *The History of the Britons* there is a separate work entitled *De Mirabilibus Britanniae* ('Concerning the Marvels of Britain'). This lists a series of miraculous events said to occur in the island, many of them concerning rivers, lakes and fountains. It is tempting to believe that they represent very ancient traditions dating from pre-Christian times, when such places were thought to be haunted by gods and demons. Even today traces of these beliefs survive. In Derbyshire, for example, there is an annual well-dressing ceremony during which wells and springs are decorated with flowers. Perhaps we may take the marvels described in this work as descriptions of those places in Britain which were sacred in prehistoric days. There is, for example, said to be a warm pool surrounded by a stone wall. Men go there to wash, and if a man wishes for cold water the pool will be cold; if he wishes for warm water it will be warm. There are also springs of salt water from which salt can be extracted; this is far from the sea and the springs come from the ground.

Arthur's name is linked with two of the marvels. In the region called Buelt there is a cairn of stones. The stone on the top of the cairn bears a dog's footprint. This was impressed by 'Cabal, the dog of Arthur the soldier' when he hunted Troynt the boar.

> Thereafter Arthur gathered together a heap of stones beneath the stone upon which was his dog's footprint; and it is called Cairn Cabal. And men come and take away the stones with their hands for a while day and a whole night, but on the following morning the Cairn can be seen again rebuilt.

The hunting of the great boar Troynt takes us straight back to Celtic mythology. The origins of the story are probably far older than the tales of Arthur. It is interesting to note that Arthur is referred to quite simply as 'Arthur the soldier'.

The other miracle to which his name is attached is said to take place in the region called Ercing:

> There is there a tomb close to a spring which is called Licat Anir, the name of the man who is buried in the mound. Anir was the son of Arthur the soldier and he himself killed him there and buried him.

The point of this marvel is that no man can measure the tomb. Sometimes it is six feet in length, sometimes nine and sometimes fifteen. However often you measure it you will never find the same dimensions, 'and I have tested this' the writer adds. Here again Arthur is simply 'the soldier'. This argues the antiquity of the passage, which was written before the legends surrounded his name and before he was known as 'King' Arthur. Tradition tells us that in the Battle of Camlan where he died, he was fighting against his own nephew. Does this marvel embody a true account of something that really happened in those troubled days? Was Arthur opposed not only by his nephew, but did his own son become his enemy in the civil wars, and did Arthur slay him?

Among marvels of shores without a sea, of rivers and of magical tombs, there is one about a spring called Finnaun Guur Helic in the region of Cinlipluc; no river flows into the spring, and no river leaves it. Men go to fish there from all the points of the compass. The words which Nennius used to describe the compass points are revealing. In the original Latin the passage reads:

> Alii vadunt in fontem ad partem orientis et deducunt pisces ex ea parte. Alii ad dextram, alii ad sinistram, ad occidentemque, et trahunt pisces ab unaquaque parte.
> (Some men go into the fountain at the eastern side and draw up fish from that side. Others go to the right, others to the left, some to the west, and they take fish from every side.)

While the classical terms are used for east and west (*orientis* and *occidentem*), the other two directions are described as 'left' and 'right'. The *History* of Nennius offers a clue as to which means north. Speaking of the Picts he tells us that they occupied the 'left hand' areas of Britain. Left therefore means north and right south. In other parts of the work, the word 'left' is used in the same way. Ancient maps were frequently drawn with the east at the top of the page. Indeed, appended to one of the manuscripts of Nennius a circle is drawn to show how the sons of Noah divided the world. Taking the form of a typical T-O map, it is bisected by a horizontal band representing an ocean.

The lower semicircle is in turn divided into two quadrants by a vertical strip of water. The upper semicircle is marked 'Asia'. The left-hand lower quadrant is marked 'Europe' and the right-hand quadrant 'Africa'.

Strabo has an interesting passage which may be relevant. In defining the terms that he will use to describe countries he specifically states that the word *length* will indicate the east-west dimension and the word *breadth* the north-south dimension. Presumably he had in mind a map with the east at the top, so that the east-west dimension lay along the length of the map. The very words latitude and longitude (which were used in the classical world) are only logical on a map of this kind. On modern maps it is degrees of latitude (breadth) that give a country's length as we see it, and degrees of longitude (length) which give its breadth.

As Britain would have been drawn with east to the top, then the description which Tacitus gives of the island, in the *Agricola*, 'shaped like a double-headed axe', springs to life. There is the cutting edge from Kent to Cornwall, the narrow waist for the haft, with the north representing the other edge.

This theory is further borne out by the manner in which the Romans divided many of the provinces of their Empire. There was for example an Upper and Lower Egypt. The division does not lie between north and south but between east and west.

This theory has one important bearing on the history of Britain. As with other provinces, it was first divided into *Britannia Superior* and *Britannia Inferior*, Upper and Lower Britain, and, there has been much theorising as to their location. If the map is turned with east to the north the solution is clear. Fosse Way, the great Roman Road which runs north-east by east, diagonally from the West Country to Lincoln neatly divides Roman Britain into an upper (eastern) and a lower (western) section. The name of the road implies that it was once a frontier with a defensive *fossa* or ditch along its length. *Britannia Superior* would then be the eastern and southern parts of the island which Rome first conquered. Until the Saxon invasions it was the most peaceful part of the province. It is in this section that most of the villas lie and where Romanisation was most complete. *Britannia Inferior* contains the troubled frontier lands protected by Hadrian's Wall and the great military centres of York and Chester. The two regions are distinct and the Fosse Way is the natural frontier between them.

The works of Nennius have preserved invaluable historical material, largely drawn from the Britons' side, of the darkest and most mysterious period of Britain's history. Without him we would know little of King Vortigern and the coming of the Saxons, and still less of Arthur the soldier. And the brief addition to his work, *The Marvels of Britain*, throws unexpected light upon the geography of Roman Britain.

IV

THE ANGLO-SAXON CHRONICLE: TO AD 734

SO far, we have seen the Anglo-Saxons through the eyes of the defeated and resentful Britons. Gildas had been rendered almost incoherent by his anger at the men who had caused all the grief and desolation he saw around him. A complex civilisation, patiently built during the four centuries of Rome's authority, was being totally destroyed, and there was no room in his heart for any emotion but wrath. He could not describe, only abuse, the barbarians who had so wantonly wrought that destruction.

The compilers of the *Welsh Annals* were more resigned. In their day the Britons had accepted that their destiny now lay in the narrow confines of their new kingdoms in the west. They were less bitter than Gildas but no less hostile. Until the Anglo-Saxons became Christians they preferred to ignore their savage neighbours, content to record the passing of their bishops and the sun's eclipses. Nennius, to the extent that he drew on sixth- and seventh-century material, inherited some of the anger which smouldered in the hearts of his ancestors during those evil days.

The picture that we have, then, of the Anglo-Saxons is of a barbarous and bloodthirsty people, seeking power not justice, forcibly seizing land which of ancient right belonged to others, brutally extinguishing the Christian faith which had for so long illuminated men's lives, waging unprovoked wars like brigands,

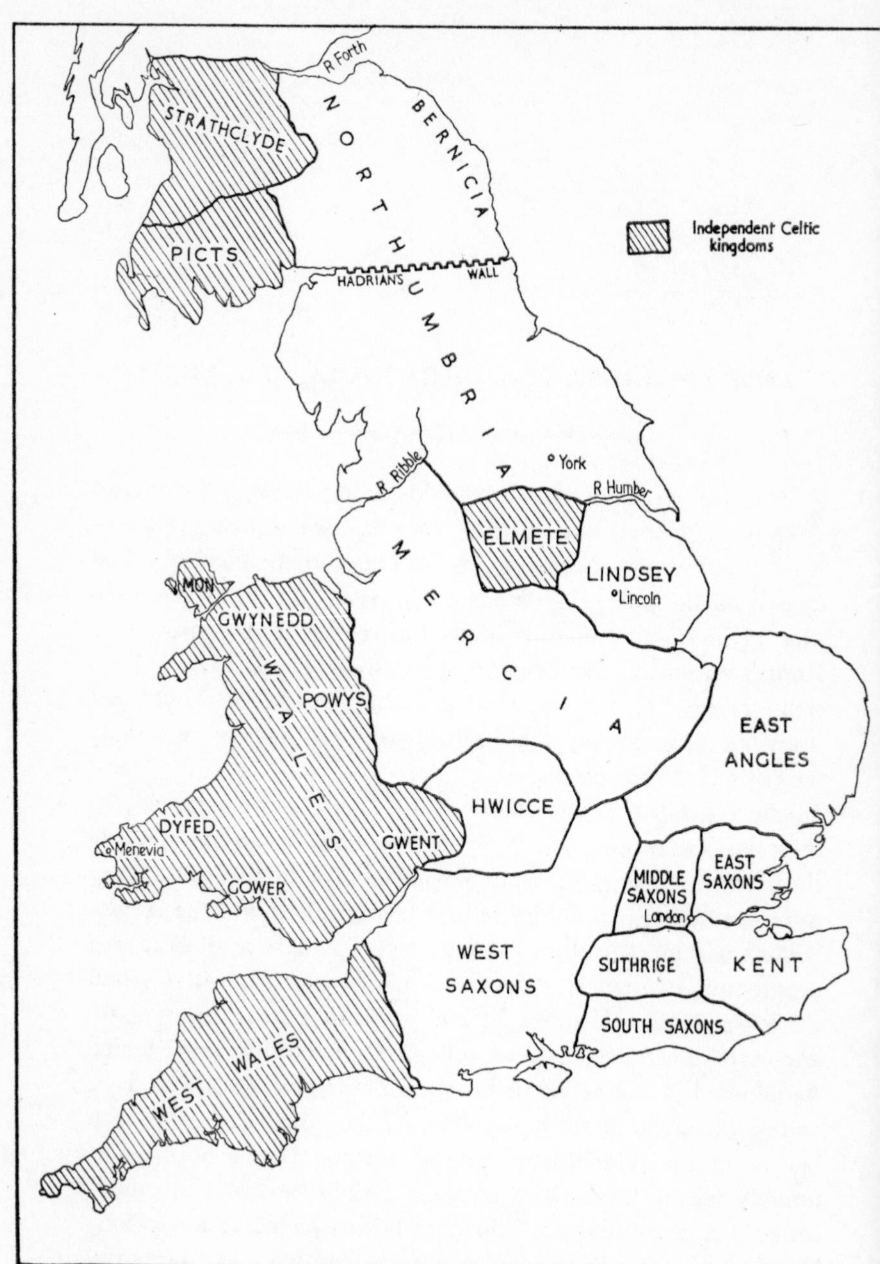

ENGLAND AND WALES c AD 700

pursuing piracy at sea and violent robbery on land, and not flinching from the blackest treachery if, by so doing, they could advance their cause or increase their booty. The story of Hengist's butchery of his guests in cold blood may be fact or fable. The important thing to remember is that the Britons believed it to be true and that Nennius could record it many centuries later as factual history.

Three hundred years after Hengist's day we see, through the eyes of the Britons, the violent lust for power of King Penda of Mercia. The Britons who allied themselves with him did so in an attempt to destroy the Saxons in Northumbria, their hereditary enemies. For them the alliance was logical and consistent with their unrelenting purpose. But they must have looked with some scorn on Penda's alliance as typical of the Saxons' obsession with conquest. He was treacherously waging war on his own kinsfolk at a time when they were under heavy attack from the Britons.

Ruthless the Anglo-Saxons certainly were, greedy for power in the decaying Roman province and for the fine farmland they found there. But they had other qualities which the Britons could hardly be expected to appreciate. They were fine craftsmen in gold and enamel. They had a sense of discipline and loyalty to their captains. Their society was ordered by strict rules and customs which they would later codify into law. Coming as they did from Germany, which Roman armies had never permanently penetrated, and where Mediterranean civilisation was therefore never planted, the first generations in Britain were largely illiterate. They had a great sense of the past and, long before they were able to maintain written records, they celebrated the deeds of their dead kings and heroes in songs that were sung from age to age. They took pride in the ancestry of their kings and kept records (initially verbal, perhaps) of their descent. Their poems were alliterative. Kings give their sons names which began with the same letter as their own, no doubt to assist in the composition of songs celebrating the royal house, so that Cenred was the son of Ceolwold, son of Cutha, and so on back to Cerdic, the first king of the West Saxons.

At some early period they began to record, either in writing (which they learned in Britain) or verbally, the notable events that occurred during their conquest of the island. Later, after Christianity came to them, and with it a knowledge of Latin and access to the works of Roman and Romano-British writers, these early traditional records were embodied into formal annals. Thereafter the most notable events of each year until the twelfth century were recorded, and it is this series of documents which is known as the *Anglo-Saxon Chronicle*.

The *Chronicle* is unique in many ways. Although the earliest section may have been partly based on Latin documents, the *Chronicle* itself is written in English. The results were far-reaching. Brief annual entries develop into a full narrative of the most important occurrences in each year, and the authors gradually develop a prose style. The direct and lucid manner in which they summarise events gave the English language, very early in its history, a clarity and directness which it has never lost.

The *Chronicle* is extraordinarily complete. From the end of the sixth century, there are entries for almost every year. This would be consistent with the suggestion that the *Chronicle* as we know it was first compiled by Christian monks. St Augustine brought Christianity to the English in 597. Very soon thereafter King Aethilberht of Kent produced a written code of laws which imposed fines for the theft of property from bishops, priests, deacons and clerks. These laws show how quickly the Anglo-Saxons made use of the art of writing and how quickly the various orders of clerics were established.

There is some evidence that the first section of the *Chronicle* was written after Aethilberht's death in 616. In 565, we are told, 'Aethilberht succeeded to the kingdom of Kent and ruled fifty-three years.' (The discrepancy of two years is not important.) We are also told that during his reign Gregory sent Christianity to the English. This was evidently not written until Aethilberht had died. Certainly from about 616 the entries become increasingly complete and have a contemporary ring.

The *Chronicle* is remarkable for the accuracy and detail of its entries. From the seventh century onwards, the full narrative for many of the years contrasts dramatically with the clipped sentences of the *Welsh Annals*. In many cases we seem to be reading eyewitness accounts, and we can imagine soldiers and nobles telling the monks of the battles and other great events that had taken place outside the tranquil monasteries. It is as though the compilers knew that they were writing for posterity and were anxious to give as full a narrative as possible. There are occasional errors in dating, which spring from simple causes—when copies were made the scribe could easily err in copying the Roman numerals. Again, where there were blank years between entries, a copyist could easily omit one of these and so throw the reckoning out by a year. Apart from such natural blunders, there is another reason for not always being able to assign events to the correct year—many different dates were used to mark New Year's Day. The Romans had taken March as the first month of the year, for this was the time of the spring equinox and of the renewal of life in farmland and forest. Our months of September, October, November and December are memorials of this, for they are the seventh, eighth, ninth and tenth months of a year which begins in March. Then, every fifteen years the Romans reviewed the tax assessments in September. These fifteen-year periods (known as Interdictions) continued to be used in the chronological scheme of the church, so that a date in September was sometimes taken as New Year's Day. Finally, Christian festivals—the Annunciation (25 March) and the Nativity (25 December) were also used. Within these limits, though, the *Chronicle* is remarkably accurate.

Its continuity is extraordinary, for in one form or another it was maintained until 100 years or more after the Norman conquest. In one monastery, the same book was used for 200 years.

The first Christian compilers of the *Chronicle* set out to collect all that was known about Britain from the time of Julius Caesar's invasion until their own day, after which the contemporary annual records could begin. They included world events in the earliest section—the accession of Roman emperors and the growth of Christianity. Four separate sources can be distinguished: the Bible, Roman authors, the writings of the Britons, and finally the older traditions (written or oral) of the Anglo-Saxons themselves.

The *Chronicle* opens, in a manner reminiscent of Nennius, with a brief description of Britain. Five languages spoken in the island are listed—English, British or Welsh, Irish, Pictish and Latin. We then have a brief account of the coming of the Britons from Britanny and of the Picts from Scythia.

Then follows an excellent summary of Julius Caesar's two invasions, clearly based on Caesar's own writings. It contains only two errors: the date is given as 'sixty years before Christ was born', and Caesar, on his return to Gaul after his first unsuccessful expedition, is said to have left his army 'among the Irish'. The author's Latin was a little shaky: he has mistranslated Caesar's word *hiberna* (winter quarters) for *Hibernia* and so sends the Roman army off to Ireland instead of into their barracks for the winter! For the rest it is admirably done and contains none of the wild blunders of Nennius.

After this there is a series of Biblical entries, beginning with the birth of Christ 'in the forty-second year' of the reign of Octavian. The Slaughter of the Innocents, Christ's baptism and crucifixion, and martyrdom of Stephen, and Paul's conversion are among the matters recorded.

We are told of the conquest of Britain by Claudius in two brief sentences, and that Nero succeeded to the kingdom, and lost the island of Britain. In fact he did not, though it was during his reign that Queen Boudicca's swift and savage revolt almost succeeded in destroying Roman rule. This entry in the *Chronicle* (unlike the accounts of Caesar and Claudius) was not drawn from classical sources, but seems rather to echo a British tradition, for Nennius made a similar statement about Nero.

The *Chronicle* then records the martyrdom of Peter and Paul, the succession of Vespasian, the sack of Jerusalem, and the accession in turn of Titus and Domitian. In 167, we are told, 'Lucius, King of the Britons, sent men to Rome to ask for baptism.' Here the writer is repeating Nennius almost word for word. The date is the same, but the *Chronicle* corrects the name of the pope to whom Lucius sent his messengers from Evaristus, as given by Nennius, to Eleutherius who held the papal see in 167. The *Chronicle* also adds that the Britons remained Christian until the reign of Diocletian. Clearly the first compiler of the *Chronicle* had available either the works of Nennius or the same sources, but the Saxon writer was a more precise scholar than Nennius. We can imagine him checking through the list of popes and making his correction with a smile of satisfaction and a consciousness of his superiority over the Briton whose work he was using. We can see the same careful approach in his mention of Diocletian, during whose reign Christianity was rigorously persecuted. It was a fairly safe deduction that the faith perished in Britain. In fact it did not.

Against 286 the martyrdom of St Alban is noted, and this, too, must have been derived from a British source. There is a brief account against 380 of Maximus, the ambitious officer who led the Legions out of Britain, caused the death of Gratian, captured Rome and became Emperor. The account contains several inaccuracies. It records that Maximus was born in Britain whereas he was a Spaniard. It is said that he was conquered by Valentinian, whereas in fact he was defeated at Aquileia by Theodosius. All this suggests that the author was working not from a Roman but a British source.

The fall of Rome to the Goths is recorded in 409; the *Chronicle* adds that after this date the Kings of the Romans no longer ruled in Britain. Roman rule had, in fact, begun to wither twenty-seven years earlier when Maximus stripped the island of its garrison. This use of Rome's capture to mark the end of her rule in Britain has given rise to a myth which still lingers in our history books. The deduction was made that the Legions left to rescue the Eternal City, beset as she was by the barbarian armies. Romantic books and plays are still written of the Legions' reluctant and gallant departure from their island home, to march to the defence of Rome. The reality of their departure under the selfish and ambitious Maximus is forgotten. Forgotten too is the fact that a quarter of a century before the Goths seized Rome, they (the Britons) had captured it, hailing their leader as Emperor. Such is the enduring force of one brief sentence, and such is the responsibility of historians!

Then, in 443, the *Chronicle* takes up the story of the coming of the Anglo-Saxons. This entry is based on a British source, for it tells the story from the Britons' point of view, recounting how they appealed to Rome and asked for soldiers against the Picts. But the source is not Gildas, for it adds one detail upon which he is silent: the Romans had no legions to send because they were fighting Attila, King of the Huns. This addition sounds authentic because we know that Aetius (to whom Gildas tells us the appeal was addressed) did in fact lead a campaign against the Huns. Nor is Nennius the source. The *Chronicle* tells us that the Britons then appealed to the Angles for help, whereas Nennius tells us that the help of the Angles was sought *after* some of them had already landed in Kent as exiles from Germany. It appears that the composers of the *Chronicle* may have had access to another British source, now lost.

The next entry (449) is evidently based upon some other work. It refers the events to the reign of 'Mauricus' (an error for Marcian) and Valentinian, adding that 'it was during their time' that Vortigern invited the Angles to Britain, and they came in three ships. This looks like Gildas again. But intermingled with the story is another tradition, probably Saxon, for the name of the place where they landed is given as *Heopwinesfleot*—Ebbsfleet in Pegwell Bay, Kent. There is still further information, probably added after the time of Bede (whose *History* we shall shortly examine); we are told that the invaders came from three nations of Germany: the Saxons, the Angles and the Jutes. This detail cannot have come from any British source contemporary with the first landings, for Hengist's men were from one nation only; almost certainly it is derived from Bede, and through him from an Anglo-Saxon tradition.

From this time onwards the *Chronicle* is clearly based on the traditions of the invaders. The names of the places where battles were fought are given. There was an engagement at Ægelesthrep (Alysford) in 455 and another in the following year at Crecganford (Crayford), after which the Britons 'fled in great fear to London'. There, protected by the strong Roman walls, the army of the Britons must have found a safe if crowded refuge, and had time to rest and refit. There is silence for nine years, but in 465 Hengist and his son Aesc (called Octha by Nennius) fought the Britons again at Wippedesfleot.

The year 473 seems to have marked a climax in the first campaign of Hengist against the Britons: 'In this year Hengist and Æsc fought with the Welsh and took much plunder, and the Welsh fled from the English like fire.' Gildas had used the same metaphor of fire to describe the advance of the invaders when they broke out of Kent and swept deep into Britain.

The pace of events now quickens. In 477 a new leader, Aelle, with his three sons Cymen, Wlencing and Cissa, landed with three ships. They slaughtered many Britons and drove them into the thick forest of the Weald. Eleven years later Hengist died and Æsc became King of Kent.

On a shelving shore from which the sea has now retreated, in what is now the county of Sussex, the Romans had established one of the finest of their shore defences. Round it they built stone walls with bonding courses of neat red brick, their massive defences reinforced by great bastions. The Romans called it the fort of Anderida; today it bears the name of Pevensey. The huge walls still stand, save for a short stretch to the south, where they have tumbled in some forgotten landslide. Queen Elizabeth I's men mounted cannon there to guard the coast from the Spaniards. In the 1940s guns were again placed there against the threat of invasion. The *Chronicle* records that in 491 Aelle and Cissa attacked this fortress, and slew all who were within: 'not one Britain was left there'.

More adventurers landed four years later—Cerdic and his son Cynric, with five shiploads of men. Cerdic (whose name seems not to be Saxon, and who may have been descended from some British emigrant settled on the Continent) later became king of the West Saxons and is the ancestor of the present royal house of England. Then, in 508, Cerdic and Cynric slew a British king 'whose name was Natanleod and 5,000 men who were with him'.

Not all the entries are reliable. Five thousand dead is an impossible figure for the last battle mentioned. Some of the events even seem to have been invented in an attempt to explain place names. In 501 a man named Port is said to have come with two ships to Portsmouth! Thirteen years later, it is reported, the West Saxons arrived under their leaders Stuf and Wihtgar, who was given the Isle of Wight in 534. For the most part, though, the record rings true and gives a clear and acceptable picture, year by year, of the advance of the Anglo-Saxons and the establishment of their kingdoms.

We have seen from the records of the Britons that they won a great victory at the Battle of Badon, in 517. Gildas tells us a golden age of peace and prosperity followed for the Britons, which lasted until the generation which fought the battle had died, and memory of the deliverance faded.

The *Chronicle* does not mention Badon, yet the results of that battle seem to be reflected in it. After the battle in 508 when the British king Natanleod was killed, the *Chronicle* claims no inland victory until 552 (the capture of the Isle of Wight in 534 took place on the periphery of Britain's defences). In 552 Cerdic's son Cynric defeated the Britons at Salisbury. So for thirty-five years after Badon the Saxons made no significant advance, and the Britons enjoyed some respite. It was only after a period long enough for a new and thoughtless generation to come to power, that the defences of the Britons failed, and the armies of the Saxons surged westwards.

In 519, two years after Badon, the *Chronicle* records that 'Cerdic and Cynric took the kingdom of the West Saxons.' It does not seem altogether fanciful to believe that the West Saxons, disorganised and dispirited after Badon where they had suffered such severe casualties, were at this time seeking new and more effective leadership. Here we may be seeing the effects of the Britons' overwhelming victory.

In 547, the year of Arthur's death and a time of civil war among the Britons, the *Chronicle* makes its first reference to Northumbria. The British defences now lay in ruins, and English kingdoms were being established in the north and the south.

In 565 we are told of Aethilberht of Kent, and in 597 of the coming of St Augustine to preach Christianity to the English. By now the new English kingdoms were struggling with one another for power, and in 568 the West Saxons drove Aethilberht back into his kingdom of Kent, from which he had marched to attack them.

The West Saxons—the men of Wessex—were now the spearhead of the English advance into British territory. In 571 they captured Limbury in Bedfordshire, Aylesbury in Buckinghamshire, and Eynsham and Benson in Oxfordshire. So for 150 years the Britons had held their enemies in the east. But six years later, though, the West Saxons took Gloucester, Cirencester and Bath, and the Britons, as a nation, were now virtually confined to Wales, the only part of the island which they still hold to this day.

Their resistance had been magnificent. For close on 150 years they had fought resolutely against their enemies, and they were to continue the struggle for many more years in the north. The myth of their swift retreat to Wales—defenceless refugees who had forgotten the art of war during the Roman occupation—has gained too great a credence. The mournful tale of Gildas is perhaps responsible for its birth. The *Anglo-Saxon Chronicle*, written by their enemies whose kinsfolk had known the bite of their swords and the stubbornness of their fighting line, helps to destroy the unworthy legend.

With the opening of the seventh century, the *Chronicle* becomes increasingly concerned with Church matters. Augustine's appointment by Pope Gregory as Archbishop is recorded. We learn of King Aethilberht's appointment of Mellitus and Justus as Bishops of London and Rochester, of the death of Pope Gregory, and in the same year (605) of the battle at Chester where King Aethelfrith of Northumbria slew 'a great number of the Welsh'. As to whether he also butchered numerous unarmed monks (which we have read in the British accounts of the battle), the *Chronicle* is silent. Remembering that the author was, like King Aethelfrith, an Englishman, but that, like the king's victims, he was a Christian, we can imagine the conflict of loyalties that held back his pen.

We are told of the growing strife between the English kingdoms. In 626 an agent of Wessex tried to assassinate King Edwin of Northumbria. The agent, Eomer, stabbed Edwin but only succeeded in wounding him and two of his thanes. Edwin, himself a pagan, had married a Christian, daughter of King Aethilberht of Kent; she had brought Paulinus, a priest, to be her chaplain. On the night of the attempted assassination, she gave birth to a daughter. The wounded king told Paulinus that he would give his daughter to God if Paulinus could by prayer ensure the overthrow of the King of Wessex, who had sent the assassin. We can imagine the turmoil in the king's house, with men dressing the wounds of the king and his two thanes, and the queen, heavy with the child she was carrying, distraught by the danger her husband had undergone. Finally her labour pains begin, and she is taken to her bedroom by her women. The king, anxious for her safety, and full of anger at the man who so nearly killed him and so endangered the queen and her child, refuses to be comforted by Paulinus and demands only revenge.

His wishes were fulfilled. He led his army into Wessex where he slew five kings and a great number of men. He kept his promise and the baby was baptised.

In the following year Edwin, apparently convinced of the efficacy of Christian prayer, was himself baptised—some say by Paulinus, some say by Ruin, son of the British hero Urbgen. Afterwards Edwin appointed Paulinus to the See of York, which had lain vacant since the days when the Christian Britons held it, and Northumbria, like Kent, now became a Christian kingdom.

The results were dramatic. The men of Northumbria swiftly absorbed the scholarship and learning that were the accompaniments of the new religion. Meanwhile Northumbria came close to destruction. King Penda of Mercia, a pagan, made common cause with 'Cadwallon', King of the Britons (whom we know as Cadwalla), and the *Chronicle* records that Edwin's army was defeated by this alliance, and he himself slain, in 633. Northumbria was laid waste by the triumphant armies. Paulinus, faithful to his charge, took Edwin's widow by sea to Kent, where he was made Bishop of Rochester.

The *Chronicle* records further attacks by Penda on Northumbria. In 641 he defeated and killed King Oswald, Edwin's successor, but in 654, Penda himself was killed in battle by King Oswy of Northumbria 'and thirty princes with him and some of these were kings'; we know from the British documents that some of them were kings of the Britons. This, according to the *Chronicle*, was the Battle of Winwidfeld; Nennius says it was the Battle of Gai.

With the death of Penda the fortunes of Northumbria revived. His son Peada, who succeeded him, became a friend to King Oswy. Unlike his father he was a Christian; the *Chronicle* records that 'he and Oswy, King Oswald's son, said that they wished to found a monastery to the glory of Christ and in honour of St Peter. And they did so and named it *Medehamstede* because there is a spring there called Medeswael.' The building was entrusted to a monk named Seaxwulf. In 656 Peada died and his brother Wulfhere, who succeeded him on the throne of Mercia, continued the work 'for love of his brother Peada, for love of his sworn brother Oswy, and for love of the abbot Seaxwulf'. The *Chronicle* also records that he gave his patronage to the monastery 'according to the advice of all his wise men, both clerical and lay, who were in his kingdom'. (This is the first reference in the *Chronicle* to the king's council, and shows how old is the tradition in England of government 'by and with the advice and consent of the lords spiritual and temporal'.) When the building was consecrated, the king 'stood before all his thanes' and declared that he had endowed the monastery with broad lands. The *Chronicle* gives a very detailed account, with verbatim reports of the King's speeches, and lists the witnesses to the King's formal conveyance of the land. In dedicating the monastery to St Peter, the King said that it should be subject only to Rome and that any man who could not make the pilgrimage to Rome should visit St Peter there. The name of the place was later changed to *Peter's burh*. Today the town which grew up around the monastery is known as Peterborough.

The kingdom of Wessex continued its aggressive policy towards the Britons on its western frontier. In 658 King Cenwalh of the West Saxons is reported to have driven the Britons as far as the River Parrett in Somerset. After a few entries dealing with a war between Wessex and Mercia, we are told that in 669 'King Egbert gave Reculver to Bass, a priest, that he might build a church there.' Reculver was the old Roman fort of Regulbium which guarded the north of the channel dividing the Isle of Thanet from the Kentish mainland. In Vortigern's day it had stood as a silent and threatening sentinel over the approaches to the island; now the English nation, which had once been dominated by the Roman fort, was building a church within its massive walls. The foundations of this church are still to be seen.

War flared again between Wessex and Mercia, and King Wulfhere died in 675 after a battle with King Aescwine of

Wessex. Wessex continued her attacks on the Britons, and the *Chronicle* reports that in 682 Centwine of Wessex drove the Britons as far as the sea.

Between 685 and 688 we are told of a Wessex king named Caedwalla who invaded Kent, made a pilgrimage to Rome, and there died a week after being baptised by the Pope. This is the king who was confused with King Cadwalla of the Britons by the compiler of the *Chronicle of the Princes of Wales.*

The eighth century opens with the accession of Coenred to the Kingdom of Mercia; the first few entries are concerned with Church matters. In 710 Ine, King of Wessex, fought against Geraint, King of the Britons. In 722 there is a record of a military expedition led by a woman—Aethelburh, wife of King Ine, who sacked Taunton. In 726 King Ine abdicated and went to Rome, an event which reminds us that communications with the Continent were now open. In 734 'the moon appeared as if it were steeped in blood, and Tatwine and Bede died'.

The *Anglo-Saxon Chronicle* has by now reached something very close to perfection. Entry after entry describes both religious and secular events clearly and accurately.

Before we continue our examination of the *Chronicle*, however, we will turn to the works of Bede, who, though neither abbot nor bishop, was considered worthy of mention in it; we shall see how he earned himself a place in the story.

V

BEDE'S ECCLESIASTICAL HISTORY OF THE ENGLISH PEOPLE

IN about 673 a boy was born near the recently-founded monastery at Wearmouth, now Monkswearmouth, in Northumbria. Christianity was new in that northern kingdom. Edwin, its first Christian king, had been baptised a mere forty-five years before, so that old men could still remember the days when Woden and Thor were worshipped and when the priests of those ancient gods had held honourable places in the king's council.

But the new faith swiftly took root and flourished. The building of the great monastery at Peterborough was followed by the foundation of other houses. At Wearmouth, as at Peterborough, the monastery was dedicated to St Peter, and it, too, was endowed with land. It was on these church lands that the boy was born; his father, a tenant of the monastery, would have visited it regularly to pay his rent. He would have seen the monks working in the fields, reading and writing in the bright new building, and heard them singing the choral offices.

When the boy was seven his parents sent him as a pupil to the monastery, entrusting him to the learned Abbot Benedict. Shortly afterwards Bede, for such was the lad's name, was moved from Wearmouth to Jarrow, where a new monastery dedicated to St Paul had been founded. Here his education was supervised by Abbot Ceolfrid. Bede did not completely lose touch with his old tutor Benedict, for he had founded the new monastery and continued to govern both Wearmouth and Jarrow. Benedict had been educated on the Continent, had visited Rome, and came to Britain with Theodore when the Pope appointed Theodore Archbishop of Canterbury in 669. Benedict was a man of many parts, learned in both Latin and Greek, and able to lecture on astronomy and music as well as on more orthodox church topics. He was especially interested in architecture and music, and brought builders from Gaul to instruct the native craftsmen. He also brought a singer from Rome so that his monks might learn to sing their offices 'as it was done at St Peter's', wrote Bede.

Bede himself was a gifted singer. He later wrote that he sang the choral offices daily in church.

The kingdom of Northumbria suffered a major disaster in 685 when Bede was about twelve years old. King Ecgfrith of Northumbria had ridden north with his army to ravage the lands of the Picts, who made as if to retreat before the onslaught of the English; King Ecgfrith's army fell into the trap. They pursued their enemy into a narrow glen with steep sides. There the Picts attacked. King Ecgfrith was killed with most of his men. This was the Battle of Dunnichen Moss which Bede himself described in his *History*.

> After which, both the hopes and the power of the English kingdom began to weaken and to sink back. For the Picts recovered again their old lands which had been taken by the English. The Scots who dwelt in Britain, and also a number of the Britons obtained their freedom again, which they have continued to hold for forty-six years.

Young Bede would have seen the shaking of heads when news of this crushing defeat reached the monastery, and heard mournful criticisms of the dead king's rashness. The year before, Ecgfrith had sailed with his army to Ireland, much to the disgust of Bede's elders. Churchmen had considered the king's expedition reckless and wrong. The Irish were Christians, and had never harmed the English. Worse, Ecgfrith sacrilegiously destroyed Irish churches and monasteries. Bede himself was to be very critical of Ecgfrith in his *History*. Now the king, in attacking the Picts, had acted directly against the advice of his council, and in particular against that of Bishop Cuthbert.

We know the name of the victorious Pictish leader, for it is recorded in an Irish chronicle, the *Annals of Tigernach*. The Irish annalist, remembering Ecgfrith's savage campaign in Ireland during the previous year, must have noted with some satisfaction the revenge which fate had brought:

> Battle of *Duin Nechtain* [the Fort of Nechtain] on May 20th, a Saturday, in which *Ecgfrid mac Osu* [Ecgfrith son of Oswin] king of the Saxons, having reigned fifteen years, was slain with a great company of his soldiers by Bruidhi son of Bili, king of Fortrenn.

But wars and the loss of armies were not the only disasters to be feared in seventh-century Northumbria. The anonymous *Life of Abbot Ceofrid* records that in 686 there was an epidemic in the Jarrow monastery. All those who could read, preach or recite the antiphons or responses died except the Abbot himself and

> one boy whom he had brought up and taught, and who is now a priest in the same monastery, and who commends the worthy deeds of the Abbot, both in writing and by word of mouth to all who wish to learn about him.

This boy is usually taken to be Bede himself. The supposition is entirely logical, for we know that Bede survived the epidemic, dying when he was in his sixties, and that he was a boy of about thirteen at the time of the plague. Moreover, Bede remained at Jarrow all his life as a monk, and was the author of a biography of Ceofrid in which he certainly commended the worthy deeds of the Abbot.

The account of the plague goes on to describe how Ceofrid, greatly upset by all that had happened, ordered that the few who were left should abandon their former ceremonies and recite the psalms without antiphons, except at Vespers and Matins. After a week, however, the Abbot could bear it no longer and ordered that the customary antiphons should be restored.

> All helped; and by means of himself and the boy of whom I have spoken, carried out with no small labour what he had ordered, until he could train others to help in the Divine Service, or obtain them from elsewhere.

A boy of thirteen able to carry out this task in the stricken monastery was clearly a lad of outstanding ability. When we remember Bede's statement that he sang the choral offices every day of his life, right up to the time when he was approaching sixty, the identification seems certain.

Six years later, when he was nineteen, Bede was ordained deacon by Bishop John, on the recommendation of Abbot Ceofrid. When he was thirty he was ordained priest, again by Bishop John, and again under the direction of Ceofrid. He himself wrote:

> I have spent all the rest of my life in this monastery, applying myself throughout to studying the scriptures. I have followed the regular discipline and have sung the choir offices every day in the church. But my greatest pleasure always has been in studying, in teaching and in writing.

Bede lived until he was just over sixty, having spent more than half a century pusuing his scholarly ambitions. He was active until the very end, working among his beloved books and dictating to within a few minutes of his death. He was the author of some forty works, including translations, biographies, commentaries on books of the Old and New Testaments, a treatise on chronology and—his greatest achievement—the *Ecclesiastical History of the English People*.

Among those working and studying with him was a young man named Cuthbert (not to be confused with the great St Cuthbert) who later became Abbot of Jarrow and Wearmouth. He was present when Bede died and wrote a very full account to a friend, Cuthwin, who had asked for details. The account takes us into Bede's cell, where we can ourselves be present at the last tranquil scene of his busy life.

About a fortnight before Easter, wrote Cuthbert, Bede grew weaker and began to have difficulty breathing. He had no pain and continued quite cheerful and contented until Ascension Day. He was still giving lessons every day to his students, and (more evidence of his love of music) spent much of his time singing the Psalms. He knew that death was near. On one occasion he quoted an English poem describing man's last journey: 'No one is wiser than he, who before setting out, considers what good and evil he has done and what doom his soul shall receive after death.' During this time he was working on an English translation of the Gospel of St John—a reminder of how ancient is the idea of an English Bible. On the Tuesday before Ascension Day he talked and dictated cheerfully. He told the young men who were with him to work quickly, adding 'I don't know how much longer I shall be with you, nor whether God shall soon summon me.' His breathing had become more difficult and his feet had begun to swell.

On Wednesday morning he worked during the early part of the day. Then all but one of the young men left him to walk in procession with the relics of the saints, as was customary on Ascension Day. The young monk said: 'There is still one chapter to be done of the book you were dictating. But it seems hard for me to question you about it now.' 'No,' said Bede, 'it is easy. Take your pen and sharpen it, and write quickly.'

He went on dictating his translation of the Gospel, in spite of his laboured breathing and increasing weakness. Then his mind wandered from his work and he remembered the one or two personal possessions which the rules of the monastery permitted him to keep. He broke off his dictation and said to the boy: 'I have a few valuable things in my chest: pepper, napkins and incense. Run along and bring the priests of the monastery so that I can distribute the gifts which God gave me.'

The young man, in great distress, went on his sad errand. When the monks came into Bede's cell, he talked to them all and asked them to offer masses and prayers for him. Most of them were weeping. But in their sorrow they were comforted by Bede himself and by his confident faith. 'It is time for me to go back to Him who made me, when I was not, out of nothing,' he said. 'I have lived long, and my merciful Judge has ordered my life pleasantly.' During the rest of the afternoon he talked happily with his friends. Then one of his students, a boy named Wilbert, said: 'Master, there is still one sentence which we have not written.' 'Well then, write it down,' answered Bede. And after a little while the boy said 'Now it is finished.' Said Bede 'Indeed, it is finished! Now raise up my head with your hands, for I would like to sit up opposite the holy spot where I used to pray, so that I may call upon my Father.' And so, sitting on the floor of his cell and singing 'Glory be to the Father and to the Son and to the Holy Ghost' he breathed his last.

His life had been one of immense achievement. It was not the mere diversity and number of the books he had written that was the measure of his greatness. It was rather his superb scholarship which, in its depth and precision, was centuries ahead of the age in which he lived. Within less than a century of the coming of Christian learning to Northumbria, here was a man who was greatly superior to men like Gildas and Nennius, the heirs to centuries of knowledge. He took vast care to collect his information and then to marshal it in an orderly and precise manner.

In his *Historia Ecclesiastica Gentis Anglorum* (*Ecclesiastical History of the English People*), which he wrote in Latin when in his fifties, Bede saw the historian's task as a social and moral one. In his preface, he pointed out that if history records the virtues of good men, then the virtuous reader is encouraged to follow the good. If it records the wickedness of evil men, then the reader will be prompted to avoid similar sins.

His methods were extremely thorough, and any modern historian would be proud to follow his example. He was at great pains to list the sources he used, so that readers might be confident about the book's authenticity. He tells us that his chief adviser (and indeed the man who suggested the work) was Albinus, Abbot of the monastery of St Peter and St Paul in Canterbury, who died before the book was finished. Bede had also consulted Hadrian, Albinus's predecessor. Through these two men he had access to the archives in and near Canterbury. Nothelm, a priest in London, acted as his intermediary with Canterbury, sending to Bede copies of all important documents as well as notes on local traditions.

Later Nothelm visited Rome, searching the Papal library for anything that might throw light on the history of Christianity among the English. He found copies of the letters which Pope Gregory had sent to Augustine in England during his mission, and other important papers. He brought back copies to Canterbury. Albinus sent him to Jarrow with all this material.

Bede also acknowledges the help he had from Bishop Daniel, Bishop of the West Saxon kingdom (Wessex). The Bishop sent information to Bede about events there and in the adjoining kingdom of the South Saxons (Sussex), together with notes on the Isle of Wight. For material about Mercia, he turned to the monastery at Lasingham whose monks also furnished information about the kingdom of the East Saxons (Essex). For the East Angles (East Anglia), Bede relied partly upon old traditions and partly upon information provided by Abbot Esi. For the kingdom of Lindsey in the north-east, he obtained written information from Bishop Cynebert. For matters nearer home, in the kingdom of Northumbria, Bede wrote that he had relied on numerous witnesses who either knew the facts or remembered them. He adds that he himself had first-hand knowledge of many of the events described.

The labour of organising the collection of all this material must have been immense. Letters had to be written, copies made of numerous and scattered documents, and Bede had to maintain contact with all his correspondents. We have to imagine Nothelm riding frequently to Canterbury, across London Bridge and down the old Roman road which was still more or less serviceable. Other messengers, including no doubt some of Bede's own students, rode on his long errands. No doubt they welcomed an escape from their quiet cloisters into the leafy beauty of the long roads, the gay landscape of farm and forest, and into the bustling and crowded streets of strange towns. They moved across the island, from kingdom to kingdom, bringing back copies of precious documents for Bede to read and sift. We can picture Nothelm crossing the Channel in the salt wind, landing in Gaul and making the long journey to Rome. At the end of each day's travelling he and his companions would have talked to their hosts (frequently monks and priests like themselves) about the purpose of their journey. In Rome, Nothelm was fortunate that the Pope had formerly been Vatican Librarian, and he would have been specially interested in Nothelm's task, and well fitted to guide and assist him.

In addition to the help which he organised from all these people, Bede also made abundant use of earlier written material. Unfortunately he did not list this, but it is obvious that he read, and borrowed from, the works of Orosius, Tacitus, Julius Caesar and others. Certainly he had a copy of Gildas and probably of Nennius as well. The monastery at Jarrow was only some fifty years old when Bede was working. The speed with which its library was built up is impressive, and shows how quickly the English people were developing their civilisation and their means of communication.

At the end of his history Bede has a chapter which almost seems to anticipate the modern dust jacket! He proudly lists his more important books, and adds a fairly detailed biographical sketch of himself.

The book itself begins with the geographical description of Britain which had almost become the standard opening of any history. Bede repeats the dimensions given by Gildas and Nennius, but adds further details. He lists the country's agricultural resources—including vines—and fisheries. He mentions hot and cold springs. Then, drawing on Gildas or Nennius, he tells us that in former days the land had twenty-eight fine cities. He mentions the four nations living in the island—English, British, Scots and Pict—and describes how the Britons and the Picts came to the country. There is also a fairly full description of Ireland.

For the Roman period, Bede makes excellent use of classical sources. He accurately summarises Julius Caesar's own account of his two expeditions to Britain. On the final conquest of Britain by the Emperor Claudius, Bede is equally precise. His narrative is not based on local traditions but is accurately drawn from Latin sources. He repeats the apocryphal story of 'King Lucius of Britain' who is said to have become a Christian in AD 156.

Towards the end of the third century, a man named Carausius was appointed commander of a fleet based on Britain and Gaul. His task was to protect the coasts against the piratical raids of the tribes of northern Germany, including the Saxons. Bede gives a good account of Carausius, of how he was suspected to be in league with the raiders, and of how he was ultimately defeated by the Roman authorities. The narrative is clearly drawn from classical sources.

For the events during the persecution of the Christians by the Emperor Diocletian, Bede apparently had access to a British document much fuller than the *History* of Gildas, which merely mentions that Alban was martyred at Verulamium. Bede repeats the full details, explaining how Alban had protected a Christian priest fleeing from the persecution. He gives an account of his trial, and of his being first flogged and then executed.

Bede goes briefly through the reigns of Constantius, his son Constantine the Great, and Gratian. He records the ambitious adventure of Maximus and his defeat at Aquileia. On all these matters, he is again working from continental sources. Next he describes the Pelagian doctrine, of which he is a bitter opponent. Perhaps his hostility is not merely that of a good churchman. Part of it may spring from the fact that Pelagius was himself a Briton; Bede, as an Englishman, had no time for the Britons! He refers to Pelagius as having spread 'his poisonous and abominable teaching'.

He mentions the capture of Rome by the Goths and, like the *Anglo-Saxon Chronicle*, chronologically links that event with the collapse of Roman rule in Britain. He then describes the overwhelming difficulties faced by the Britons. Here he follows Gildas very closely. True, he tidies up the style, giving the narrative lucidity and order, but essentially he is repeating the tale as Gildas told it. There is one modification and one vital addition: himself an Angle, Bede could not accept Gildas's statement that Vortigern invited the Saxons to Britain. Instead, he writes that Vortigern summoned 'the Angles *or* Saxons'. He then adds the completely new information that the men who came were from the three most powerful races of Germany, the Saxons, the Angles and the Jutes. He places the Jutes in Kent, the Isle of Wight, and on the mainland opposite. Modern research supports Bede in this. Archaeology shows that the first settlers in Kent had much in common with the Frankish tribes in Gaul, neighbours of the Jutes. No doubt Bede is here recording reliable local traditions, reported to him by Bishop Daniel of Wessex and his correspondents in Kent. His careful research has, in this passage, preserved priceless information which goes to the very roots of English history, and which otherwise might have been lost.

Bede then resumes the story as told by Gildas. We again meet Ambrosius, defender of the Britons and precursor of Arthur, under whose leadership the struggle against the Saxons was resumed and who 'with God's help' inflicted a defeat upon them.

It is interesting to see that in transcribing the account, Bede does not delete the pious and grateful reference to God's help, with which he, as an Englishman, would hardly have been in sympathy. In the same brief chapter he records the 'Battle of Mount Badon'. Like Gildas, his source, he makes no mention of Arthur.

Bede then inserts a full acount of Germanus, the soldier-bishop, who visited Britain in 429 to help the Britons in their wars with the Picts, and to refute the Pelagian heresy. (It is almost as though this material came to hand after Bede had begun his work, for it is out of context and interrupts the main flow of the narrative.) The section also contains a full account of the Alleluia Victory, the battle in which Germanus commanded the Britons against a mixed force of Picts and Saxons. Under his leadership the Britons ambushed their enemies, the cry of 'Alleluia' being both his army's war-cry and the signal for springing the trap. The Picts and Saxons were completely routed.

Bede now resumes the main theme, and in a short chapter summarises Gildas's description of the peace and plenty which the Britons enjoyed after Badon. He repeats Gildas's charge that, after the generation had died which remembered the former disasters, all restraints were abandoned and truth and justice utterly forgotten. He goes on

> To their other abominable crimes, which their own historian Gildas mournfully records, they added a complete failure to teach Christianity to the Saxons who now lived with them.

Then, as a patriotic Englishman, Bede expresses delight that the Britons had been guilty of this omission.

> But God graciously did not altogether neglect the people he had chosen (the Saxons) but had them in mind, sending worthier teachers of the truth to this nation so as to convert them to the faith.

To us, further removed from the events, Bede's criticism seems a little severe. The Britons would have had to possess almost divine qualities of forgiveness to have tried to convert the barbarians who had brutally dispossessed them, who had slain uncounted numbers, and who had destroyed the very fabric of civilisation almost throughout the island.

Bede omits an entire century (for which evidently there were no sources) and comes immediately to the mission of St Augustine to Kent in 597. From now on, ecclesiastical rather than secular matters predominate. He quotes in full the letter which Pope Gregory sent to the mission when, their resolution weakened by the prospect of travelling so far to work among the barbarous English, the party broke off their journey. He also quotes in full Gregory's letter to the Archbishop of Arles requesting the latter to render all assistance to the mission.

A detailed description is given of St Augustine's meeting with King Aethilberht of Kent, which seems to be based on a contemporary Kentish account. The labours of Nothelm in Rome, and the careful copies he made of the 140-year-old documents he found there, were put to good use. Bede gives us the full text of many of the letters that passed between Augustine and Pope Gregory. The former had asked for advice on various liturgical and doctrinal matters, and Bede has preserved both the questions and Gregory's reply. There is, incidentally, one letter in which the Pope warns Augustine against becoming too proud of his achievements. There is another written by Gregory to King Aethilberht, sending him presents and comfortingly predicting the end of the world. Bede records the death of Gregory, giving a short biographical sketch. It is here that Bede reports Gregory's famous pun about the young Angles whom he saw in Rome ('Not Angles but angels!').

Continuing his narrative of events in Britain, Bede paints a vivid picture of the bitter controversy between Augustine and the Christian Britons. When Augustine came on his mission, Gregory gave him full authority over all the bishops in the island. The Britons were very naturally resentful. Why should Rome, which had for so long neglected them, now presume to set over them a stranger, who had moreover cast his lot with their enemies? He dwelt among them and was building churches in the land of the hated English, who had so recently and so savagely bludgeoned the Britons from their province. Augustine invited the Britons to a conference in 603, but the meeting was fruitless and Augustine made matters no better by warning them that if they refused union with the church which he led, they would be attacked by their enemies. Since he was very close to the King of Kent, the warning must have seemed very like a threat to the suspicious Britons, and the conference broke up with nothing achieved. The Battle of Chester (of which we have read an account in the *History* of Nennius) in which the unarmed monks were slaughtered, was fought shortly afterwards. The differences between the two peoples and their churches were now written indelibly in blood.

The Britons had long been Christians. Now that Christianity had come to the English, it might have bound together the two nations whose destiny it was to share the same island. For many years, however, it served to emphasise the difference between the two nations. The Britons were not merely content, but proud, to continue their ancient practices. Over the previous hundred years, Rome had redefined and modified certain aspects of belief. The Britons, isolated by distance and the fog of war which enveloped the Continent during the fifth and sixth centuries, had heard nothing of this and continued their old ways. So did the Scots in the north, who had earlier been converted by the Britons.

In 604 Augustine died. His successor, Laurentius, addressed a letter to the bishops and abbots of the Scots, trying to persuade them to follow the Roman practices of the infant Church of the English, in particular in regard to the calculation of the date of Easter. Bede records all this, as well as a similar letter which Laurentius addressed to the Britons. Very soon, however, graver events took place in Kent which almost destroyed the new church. Aethilberht died in 616, and was succeeded by his son

1

Robertus Cotton Bruceus.

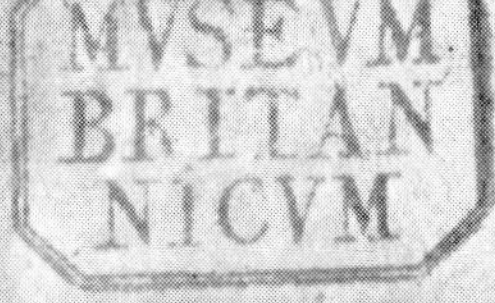

Page 117: Page from a late twelfth-century or early thirteenth-century manuscript of *Historia Britonum* by Nennius. Key, page 205.

Brittene igland is ehta hund mila lang.
7 twa hund brad. 7 her sind on þis
iglande fif geþeode. englisc. 7 brit
tisc. 7 wilsc. 7 scyttisc. 7 pyhtisc. 7
boc leden. Erest weron bugend þises
landes brittes. þa coman of armenia. 7 gesætan
suðewearde bryttene ærost. Þa gelamp hit ꝥ pyh
tas coman suþan of scithian. mid langū scipū
na manegum. 7 þa coman ærost on norþ ybernian
up. 7 þær bædo scottas ꝥ hi der moston wunian. ac
hi noldan heom lyfan. forðan hi cwædon þa scottas.
we eow magon þeah hwaðere ræd gelæron. We witan
oþer egland her be easton. þer ge magon eardian gif
ge willað. 7 gif hwa eow wið stent. we eow fultumiað. ꝥ
ge hit magon gegangan. Ða ferdon þa pihtas. 7 ge
ferdon þis land norþanweard. 7 suþanweard hit hef
don brittas. swa we ær cwedon. And þa pyhtas heom abæ
don wif æt scottum. on þa gerad ꝥ hi gecuron heora
kyne cyn aa on þa wif healfa. ꝥ hi heoldon swa lange
syððan. 7 þa gelamp hit ymbe geara rina. ꝥ scotta
sum dæl gewat of ybernian on brittene. 7 þes lan
des sum dæl geeodon. 7 wes heora heratoga reoda ge
haten. from þā heo sind genemnode dælreodi. Six
tigum wintrū ær þā þe crist wære acenned. gai' iuli'
romana kasere mid hund ehtatigū scipū gesohte
bryttene. Þer he wes ærost gewenced mid grimmum
gefeohte. 7 micelne dæl his heres forlædde. 7 þa he

Page 118: The first sheet of the *Peterborough Chronicle* of the *Anglo-Saxon Chronicle*. Key, page 206.

Eadbald who rejected Christianity. So too did the two heirs of King Saeberht, the Christian king of the East Saxons, who mocked Mellitus (appointed by Augustine as Bishop of London), demanding that they receive some of the fine white bread that was offered at Mass. In the end, Mellitus and his colleague Justus, Bishop of Rochester, left their uneasy dioceses for Gaul. Laurentius remained, converted the pagan king of Kent, and recalled the two fugitive bishops. On the death of Laurentius, Mellitus became the third Archbishop of Canterbury and was succeeded by Justus in 624.

Bede now moves on to the conversion of King Edwin of Northumbria. This was a matter of intense interest to him, since he himself was a Northumbrian and he tells the story in detail, and is obviously working on good local sources. He tells us of Edwin's baptism and of the attempt on his life by an agent of Wessex. The full texts of Pope Boniface's letters to King Edwin and his Queen Ethelberga, precious documents which must have been reverently preserved in the archives of the kingdom, are quoted.

Bede tells us how Edwin, before he became king, lived in exile, with powerful enemies plotting his death. He met a stranger who prophesied his good fortune, and this stranger was Paulinus.

Before King Edwin agreed to be baptised he consulted his council, where the matter was thoroughly debated. (Bede is again clearly working from local records and traditions; the events took place just over a hundred years before he was writing and men were still alive, when Bede was young, who had lived through them.) We are given a full report of one of the speeches; how the life of man is like a sparrow, flying out of a winter's night of snow and rain into the warmth and light of a hall. After a little while the sparrow flies out again into the darkness. Such is man upon earth. If Christianity can help to explain the unknown, it is welcome.

We are given very detailed information about the campaigns of King Caedwalla of the Britons against Edwin, in alliance with Penda, the pagan king of Mercia. The meagre British records furnish the briefest outline of these wars. Bede gives us a complete and well-ordered narrative.

But as with Kent, so with Northumbria. Edwin died in battle, slain by Caedwalla who carried his head to York and there displayed the bloody trophy in St Peter's Church. Christianity in Northumbria for a while declined. Paulinus returned with Edwin's widow to seek safety in Kent, while Northumbria was ruled by heathen kings. But Oswald, a Christian hero, succeeded to the kingdom and overthrew and slew Caedwalla on the field of Denisesburn.

Gradually all the kingdoms of the English became Christian. Bede tells of the conversion of the West Saxons, the East Angles, and the East Saxons. Mercia, so long feared by Northumbria, and so long ruled by the pagan and aggressive King Penda, was converted to Christianity in the reign of his son Peada. For Bede this growth of the faith was the heart and substance of his story. The foundation of monasteries, the appointment of bishops, the miracles by which the sick were healed—all these he recounts.

But though Christianity was becoming universal in the island by the mid-600s, it was still a divisive and not a unifying force. The controversy between the Christian Britons and the infant Church of the English had not been resolved. These differences were partly administrative and partly doctrinal. With the Britons, the monastery was the key unit and the abbot all-powerful. Bishops came under the authority of the abbots and were, so to speak, merely their representatives. All matters were organised regionally. With the English there was a strong central authority in the Archbishop of Canterbury, who was the successor to Augustine and was supreme. He selected regional bishops who carried with them the traditions and power of Canterbury. The chief outward sign of the difference between the churches was the different manner in which each calculated the date of Easter. Christ's Resurrection is, after all, the central theme of the Christian religion, and the date upon which it was to be commemorated was of vital importance. The issue seemed far less trivial then than it would now to a generation prepared to consider fixing by statute the date of the anniversary of the Crucifixion and Resurrection.

For a long while these differences were accepted as inevitable, and the two churches went their separate ways. Kent, where Christianity had first been planted among the English, was separated by many miles—indeed by the whole width of Wessex—from the nearest British Christians. Essex too was cut off from contact. It was the conversion of Northumbria that brought the two groups geographically closer, and mutual knowledge quickly sharpened and emphasised the differences. Northumbria was close to the British kingdoms of Gwynnedd and Elmet, and was frequently at war with both. There was contact by sea with Ireland, which had been converted by the Britons and where British practices were followed. Finally, Northumbria was nearer to the Scottish lands than to Kent; more than once she recruited her bishops (Aidan and Finan) from the Scots who also followed British methods and beliefs.

Bede has recorded in full detail the intricate story of these contacts, not omitting his own comments. Writing of the great Aidan, whose saintly qualities he recognises, he cannot forbear from saying that the Scot had 'an unsatisfactory knowledge as to the proper manner of observing Easter'. Nevertheless, he considered it his duty as an historian to record all that was good of Aidan, but again adds 'I neither approve nor praise his failure to celebrate Easter at the correct time.'

It was in Northumbria, where the members of the two churches had begun to work together, that the problem was finally faced and discussed. In 664 a conference was called at Whitby, the monastery ruled over by the famous Abbess Hilda. Colman, an Irishman who had succeeded Finan the Scot as Bishop among the Northumbrians, was the chief protagonist of the British or Celtic point of view, and he was supported by Hilda. On the other side was Agilbert, Bishop of the West Saxons who was on a visit to Northumbria, and Wilfrid, 'a most learned man' who had studied on the Continent and at Rome itself. King Oswy of Northumbria, who presided, followed the British church in all matters. He had been converted and baptised by the Scots and spoke their language fluently.

Bede reports the debate, and obviously had read the official records. The king opened the proceedings by emphasising the need to find agreement, and told the synod that its task was to decide which set of traditions—British or Roman—was the truer. After a long discussion, Wilfrid clinched the argument by advancing the authority of St Peter, first Bishop of Rome, whose successors must surely be the repositories of the truth. He quoted 'Thou art Peter, and upon this rock I will build my Church; and the gates of hell shall not prevail against it. And I will give unto thee the keys of the kingdom of heaven'. Colman could not contend that St Columba, whose authority he claimed, could stand against St Peter. King Oswy gave his ruling: the Roman methods were to prevail.

The Synod of Whitby marked a new chapter in English history. Thenceforward the Church was to be an institution which sought to unite not only the warring kingdoms of the English, but also to bring the Britons and the Scots into some kind of uniformity with the English. Colman himself left Britain, says Bede, taking with him all the Scots whom he had taken to Lindisfarne together with some thirty Englishmen whom he had trained there as monks.

There was a further Synod in 670 at Hertford at which representatives from the kingdoms of East Anglia, Kent, Northumbria, Mercia and Wessex met under the chairmanship of Theodore, Archbishop of Canterbury, and agreed upon ten regulations for all to obey; amongst them bishops were not to interfere with one another's dioceses, monks should not wander from monastery to monastery, nor priests leave the diocese in which they worked without permission.

Ten years later Abbess Hilda died and Bede inserted a full biographical note. Her monastery at Whitby provided five bishops and Caedmon, the first English poet to have his name recorded; Bede tells us that a monk at Whitby had great skill in turning passages of the scriptures into English alliterative poetry. He was a stable-boy who, until he was old, had no knowledge of verses or songs, and when the harp was passed round at feasts so that each guest might sing, would go home. On one such occasion he returned to the stables where he worked and lay down to sleep. He dreamed that an angel appeared and asked him why he had left the feast. Caedmon explained, and the angel told him to sing a song. He found that he could, and composed a song about the creation of the world.

> Then Caedmon arose from sleep and had clearly in his mind all that he had sung when sleeping. He was taken before the Abbess and after composing other verses, was admitted by her into the monastery where he made many poems on topics from both the Old and the New Testaments.

Among all these Church matters Bede also records points of secular history. He tells us of King Ecgfrith of Northumbria invading Ireland and also of his defeat and death at Dunnichen Moss. There follows a very full account of Cuthbert, Bishop of Lindisfarne, who started his religious life in the monastery of Melrose. His relics were responsible for numerous miracles. The story of King Caedwalla of the West Saxons is told, and his death in Rome a few days after his baptism in 685, the dates being somewhat different from those given in the *Anglo-Saxon Chronicle*.

Bede is now dealing with events in his own lifetime and his narrative becomes fuller and more detailed. He includes long extracts from a book by Adamnan of Iona on the Holy Places, giving us eye-witness accounts of Bethlehem, the Hill of Golgotha and the Mount of Olives as they were in the seventh century when the splendour of Constantine's buildings was still fresh.

The Picts, while Bede was a young man, moved away from

their old practices and sought to adopt the practices of the English church. About 710, King Nechtan of the Picts sent to Jarrow, to Bede's tutor the Abbot Ceolfrid, for help in establishing the new customs and beliefs. Bede was now in his late thirties, a man of scholarship as well as piety. One wonders whether he himself assisted in drafting the letter of advice which Ceolfrid sent to the king. The letter refers (without naming the work) to Plato's *Republic*, and says how happy the world would be if kings were philosophers and philosophers were kings. It then gives careful and precise instructions as to how the date of Easter is to be calculated. The arguments are based upon both Old and New Testaments. The Last Supper was the Passover Supper, so that the Law of the Passover must be observed, and Easter must fall between the 15th and 21st days of the month. (All this goes back to the days of Moses and the escape from Egypt.) But because the Resurrection took place after the Sabbath, the feast of Easter must begin on the Lord's Day. There are classical allusions to Scylla and Charybdis—and references to Theophilus of Alexandria, Cyril his successor, and to Dionysius Exiguus, all of whom had drawn up tables showing the true dates of Easter. There is an equally careful argument about the proper form of the tonsure. Lest his readers should wonder what the Pictish king made of all this erudition, Bede tells us that after the letter had been translated, the king fell on his knees and thanked God that he now understood the reasons that lay behind the true calculation of the date for Easter!

Bede then records the conversion of the community of Iona to the proper practices as regards Easter. He reproves the Britons who had not passed on to the English their knowledge of Christianity, and who were still obstinate, handicapped by their errors, and having their hair tonsured in the wrong manner! He ends his book with a note on the state of Britain in 751, the year the work was completed.

Bede's *Ecclesiastical History of the English People* is of unique importance. If all other sources had been lost—Gildas, the *Welsh*

Annals, Nennius and the classical writers—Bede's careful summary of events up to the coming of Augustine would have given us the main events of the Roman period and the coming of the Saxons. For the later period, the care with which he collected material from Rome and from all the English kingdoms, and the skill with which he used it, have left a superb account of the first 200 years of English history. Thanks to him, and to the long errands upon which he sent his messengers, a great deal is known of the rivalries and wars between the kingdoms of the English. Kent was notable as the first kingdom to receive Christianity. Wessex was oustanding for military prowess and for pushing the English frontiers far to the west. Mercia grew from a border kingdom to a powerful realm extending from the Welsh Marches to the North Sea. Northumbria provided learning of a high order and was a point of contact between the English, the Britons, the Picts and the Scots, bringing all these warring nations together within the frontiers of religion. Bede does not merely recount, but in his own person exemplifies, the speed with which scholarship and religious sensitivity spread among the English, who had been seen by their enemies only a few generations earlier as utterly barbarian, callous and evil. He is in every way—by virtue both of the methods he used, and of the care and thoroughness with which he exercised his skill—the father of English history. He was to exercise a profound effect for generations and remains to this day one of the most reliable, as he is one of the most readable, of England's historians. He tells almost all we need to know of the coming of the English into the island of Britain, of their wars, their conversion to Christianity, and of their slow transition from a group of violent and ruffianly tribesmen into a richly diverse and yet uniform nation, adding to their native skill in the arts of war a rich knowledge of the arts of peace.

VI

KING ALFRED AND THE LATER ANGLO-SAXON CHRONICLE

SOME fifty years after Bede's death, there began a series of events which nearly destroyed both the English Church and the English people, whose history he had so brilliantly recorded. By a strange irony the English, now civilised, Christian, and for the most part firmly settled into the orderly framework of farm and village, city and monastery, were to share the experience of the civilised and Christian Britons whom they themselves had once so savagely attacked and dispossessed.

Under the date 787 the *Anglo-Saxon Chronicle* noted:

> In this year King Beorhtric took to wife Eadburgh, King Offa's daughter; and in his time three ships of the Norwegians from Hörtland came for the first time. And then the King's representative rode there and sought to make them go to the royal house, because he did not know who they were. And then they killed him. These were the first ships of the Danes that came to England.

These ships were the first of many thousands which, over the next 250 years and more, were to bring wave after wave of invading Danes and Scandinavians. Like the Britons before them, the English now had to fight for possession of their homeland. Like them, they saw their churches pillaged and burned, their altars desecrated with blood, their monks slain, and the dark smoke of burning houses spreading across the clear skies of summer. Like the Britons, they could not prevent the heathen host from gaining a foothold in the island, nor from seizing large areas as their own. Now they knew what it was to be fugitives and to be harried by pagans who sailed their cruel ships deep inland, along the wide estuaries and once-peaceful rivers. Unlike the Britons, however, they were to absorb the new people into their own nation, to teach them their own language and loyalties, and ultimately to give Christianity to them.

Five years after the coming of the three ships and the slaughter of the King's reeve, the *Chronicle* reported the terrible misfortunes which now struck Northumbria. A period of thunderstorms and gales was followed by a famine; in the same year the Danish ships attacked, looted and destroyed the great monastery of Lindisfarne. 'There was much slaughter.' Behind this terse phrase we glimpse the helmeted Danes advancing triumphantly through the monastery buildings, cutting down the unarmed and praying monks with their terrible long-handled axes, eagerly snatching the treasures of gold and silver which adorned the altar and embellished the relics of the saints, and finally watching with grim satisfaction the pall of smoke that drifted over the island as they rowed their laden ships out to sea. Bede had died a mere fifty years before, and perhaps some of the monks who died that day had, as boys, seen him in his old age.

The Danish raids went on remorselessly, their fleets landing all round the shores of England, from the north-east coast of Northumbria to Devon and Cornwall. No coastal district was safe from attack, nor indeed was any inland city, for soon they were landing armies and marching deep into the English kingdoms. And now the English—like the Britons before them—were preoccupied with their own internal struggles. In 800, for example, the *Chronicle* records a battle between an *ealdorman* (or regional commander) named Aethelmund from 'the Hwicce' (in the western region of Wessex) and the men of Wiltshire led by Weohstan, also an ealdorman. The men of Wiltshire won, both leaders being killed in the fighting.

Twenty-seven years later King Egbert of Wessex conquered the kingdom of Mercia and thus became the effective ruler of all England south of the Humber. Kent, Surrey, Sussex and Essex were by now all subject to the rule of Wessex. The leadership of the kings of Wessex was to prove the salvation of the English nation and it is their descendants who now sit upon the throne of England.

In 837 no fewer than thirty-three ships' companies of Danes landed at Southampton and defeated the army of Wessex under Ealdorman Wulfheard. But later in the same year a Danish army was defeated at Portland. From now on almost every entry in the *Chronicle* is a report of the landing of whole armies by the Danes and of the resolute and unyielding defence put up by the armies of Wessex. In 855 a Danish host, moving from mere piracy to permanent settlement, spent the winter in England, occupying the Isle of Sheppey in the Thames estuary. It was clear that the raiders were now making a bid to establish a permanent kingdom in the island.

Five years later, a King Aethelberht succeeded to the kingdom of Wessex. He reigned for only six years and it was during his reign that the Danes occupied the Isle of Thanet, where the men of Hengist had been settled by Vortigern and which was thus the cradle of the English people in Britain. The Kentish men made peace with the heathens paying them money in return for peace. This must have been a time of dread and foreboding. Englishmen who knew the traditions of Hengist must have seen the coming of the Danes into Thanet and the yielding of the Kentish men as a grim reminder of their own past triumphs. Worse was to follow; the *Chronicle* reports that in 865 the heathen army broke the peace and 'marched secretly inland by night and wasted all the east part of Kent'.

When Aethelberht died, he was succeeded by his brother Aethelred. For a while the Danes switched their attacks to the north, and Wessex had some respite. For two years it was

Northumbria which suffered. The heathen host attacked York where there was a murderous battle after which the men of Northumbria, like the Kentish men, made their peace with the Danes.

In 868 the *Chronicle* reports that the King of Mercia turned for help to 'King Aethelred of Wessex and his brother Alfred' for help against a Danish army. This entry shows that Wessex was now the recognised champion of the English cause, her leadership being accepted by Englishmen beyond her own frontier, and this was to ensure the ultimate survival of the English nation. The entry is also noteworthy for its mention of King Aethelred's brother Alfred. This prince had in his youth been sent by his father to Rome and had seen with his own eyes the learning and order which survived there and of which the Church was both the repository and guardian. He was a man who had studied deeply, read widely and who passionately desired to make available to the English, in their own tongue, all the learning and tradition that was locked away in Latin. To him, although the destiny of the royal house of Wessex was to supply military leaders who wielded both sword and sceptre, the arts of peace were as dear as the more familiar glories and endurances of war. He was his brother's able lieutenant through five bloody and turbulent years.

In 871 Aethelred and Alfred led a large army to Reading and there fought a Danish host. There was much slaughter on either side and the Danes held the field. Four days later there was another pitched battle at Ashdown. Two Danish kings, Bacsecg and Halfdan, were killed as were five of their *jarls* or war leaders. The battle lasted until darkness made further fighting impossible, and the Danes were decisively beaten. A mere fortnight later they had re-formed and the king and his brother Alfred had to fight them again at Basing; this time the Danes were victorious. Two months later there was a further engagement. At first the might of Wessex prevailed and the Danes retreated, but in the end it was they who held the field, after great slaughter on either side. Later in the year, just after Easter, the king died.

He left two sons, but the men of Wessex decided that Alfred his brother should succeed him. This was no time for a boy king. The crowded events of the year, with the tired army of Wessex continually in action, demanded a seasoned captain. Alfred reigned for thirty years, dying as the tenth century dawned. His reign was magnificent, not by virtue of his victories, but rather by virtue of the extraordinary resolution he showed in defeat, and his immense achievements once victory enabled him to bring his great gifts to bear on the peaceful advancement of his kingdom.

This lay in the future. During the dark years that followed his brother's death and his own accession, it was his unyielding endeavours against the Danes, in the face of defeat and heavy casualties, that sustained and united the English nation.

By 878, five years after he had become king, all seemed lost. True, in the winter, the army of Wessex had triumphed over a Danish host in Devon, killing 800 of the enemy and capturing the flag known as 'The Raven'. The Danes looked upon this standard as both the emblem and augury of their victories. If before a battle it streamed in the wind, so that the Raven which it bore seemed to be flying, then they would prevail. But this triumph had no effect upon the main course of the war. By the spring, Alfred's armies were scattered and he himself was isolated in Somerset with only a small troop of men. There he fortified an island in the marshes, which became known as Athelney, the Prince's Island. The kingdom of Wessex—indeed the kingdom of England—was shrunk to the measure of Alfred's encampment, while the Danish host, under Guthrum their king, triumphed everywhere. But Alfred's resolution did not falter. With the men of his own small company, and with the men of Somerset round about, he continued to resist. At a time when defeat seemed total, he was still planning victory.

Throughout those dark days Alfred maintained his obstinate courage and resolve. The Danes held almost all England. The proud armies of Wessex, for so long the shield of the whole English nation, were reduced to a small remnant, hiding from their enemies. Alfred himself, like his men, had been campaigning for year after bitter year. They had met defeat more often than victory. He, like them, must have been physically weary, seeing no end to the long war against their powerful enemies, whose numbers increased each year as new fleets of dragon-prowed ships landed, bringing new armies against which Alfred's tired troops had endlessly to contend. Yet neither weariness nor the reduction of his own power diminished Alfred's resolution. From his beleaguered redoubt on Athelney he remained in communication with the neighbouring shires of his ravaged kingdom. His secret call went out to the farms and villages, and a new army was organised with which he might again move to the attack. In the words of the *Chronicle*:

> Seven weeks after Easter, he rode out of Athelney to Ecgbrytesstan, east of Selwood. All the men of Somerset and of Wiltshire, and of that part of Hampshire which is on this side of the sea, met him there and welcomed him.

We can only guess at the perilous errands of Alfred's messengers from Athelney, riding out on the king's service, and at the planning that lay behind this gathering of the men of Wessex. It was now early summer; Alfred's hopes, like the hawthorns and the hedgerows, were again blossoming. The following day he led his troops to Iley Oak, and the next day to Edington, where the Danish army was encamped in a strongly fortified position. They made their stand outside the camp and Alfred attacked. They retreated behind their fortifications, and there Alfred besieged them for two weeks before they surrendered. Under the terms of the surrender, they were to leave Alfred's kingdom, leaving hostages to ensure compliance, and Guthrum was to be baptised. Alfred himself stood sponsor at the ceremony and gave rich gifts to Guthrum.

The engagement at Edington was one of the decisive battles of English history. The defeat inflicted upon the Danes was neither overwhelming nor final. Guthrum's army was not destroyed and the Danes were to attack again and again—indeed in later years there were to be Danish kings sitting on the throne of England—but Alfred's victory at Edington put an end to Danish hopes of founding their own kingdom in the island of Britain, dispossessing the English as the latter had once dispossessed the Britons. It was because of Edington that the Danish kings who were later to rule in Britain did so as kings of England. The Danes who had settled in the farms and cities became subjects of the English crown and became integrated with the people of England.

Alfred's immense achievement in winning the desperate war, in transforming himself from fugitive captain to triumphant king, was recognised by the whole English people. In the years that preceded these events, all the English kingdoms had come to look upon Wessex as their defender. Now Wessex emerged not merely as the champion of the English, but as the only kingdom undefeated after the ordeals of invasion; it alone could provide both the military strength and the unbroken tradition for which men were looking. As a result, the king of Wessex became king of England and the true unity of the nation was forged by the arms of Alfred's men on the field of Edington. Henceforth we are concerned not with the history of Wessex, Mercia, Essex or Northumbria, but with the history of England.

The military successes of Alfred were matched by the purposeful manner in which he made use of the peace so perilously won. He was as much scholar as soldier, and made a tremendous personal contribution to the advancement of learning. After savage years of destruction—when monasteries and their libraries were looted and burned, and when men were too busy with sword and shield to turn to the writing and reading of books—Alfred looked back to those almost forgotten days when learning flourished in England, and when men like Bede were distilling into new books the knowledge and wisdom of past ages. He looked to the past not with sentimental and empty regret; he saw it rather as a challenging example and recognised that his own task was to rebuild all that the long years of war had shattered. We have his thoughts on all these matters expressed in his own words, for he translated the *Cura Pastoralis* (*Pastoral Duties*) into English, sending a copy to every bishopric in his dominions. In the preface he wrote:

> *Aelfred kyning hateth gretan Waerfreth biscep his wordum luflice ond freondlice . . .*

> Alfred the king bids greet Waerferth the bishop with his words, lovingly and in a friendly way; and I bid you know that it has very often come to my mind what wise men there once were throughout England, men both of holy and of worldly wisdom, and how happy the times were then throughout England . . . and how successful they were both in war and in wisdom; and also the men of the church, how eager they were both about learning and about teaching, and about all the laws of service that they should do for God; and how men came hither to this land from oversea to seek wisdom and learning; and how we now should seek these from outside if we should have them. Learning in England was fallen so clean away that there were very few this side of the Humber who could understand their services in English or, furthermore, who could translate a written message from Latin into English—and I think that there were not many beyond the Humber. So few were there, that I cannot think of any single one south of Thames when I took the kingdom. Thanks be to Almighty God that we now have any supply of teachers . . .
>
> When I called this to mind I remembered how I had seen, before it was all harried and burned, how the churches throughout all England stood filled with treasures and books, and also how very many were the servants of God, and they knew very little of how to use these books . . .

Alfred went on to point out that all these old books were written in Latin so that their contents were mostly inaccessible.

He therefore proposed that certain books should be translated into English, just as the Greeks had translated from the Hebrew and the Romans from the Greek. Attention should also be paid to education:

> that we should do it (as we very well may with God's help if we have peace) so that all the sons in England of free men who have means enough to follow it, should be set to learning while they may do no other duties, so that they may well know how to read written English; let those then further study Latin who are to be further taught and are marked out for higher things.

Alfred vigorously carried out the policy of translation set out in this document. Besides translating the *Cura Pastoralis* itself, he also produced an English version of the *Universal History* of Orosius, a work written in the fifth century, and so the tale of Cleopatra and other stories from the ancient world became available to the English. The reference to the survival of at least some learning north of the Humber indicates Alfred's recognition of the outstanding contribution made to scholarship by the kingdom of Northumbria in the good old days before the Danish invasions —before (in Alfred's words) all had been harried and burned. Bede's *Ecclesiastical History* was the chief monument of this northern learning, and Alfred caused an English translation to be made from the Latin. The result of all this was not merely to make available to the English people much of the learning and wisdom of past ages, but also to shape the English language into a powerful yet sensitive instrument. Although, a century and a half after Alfred's death, English was to suffer a temporary eclipse and French was to become the official language of England, it never lost the qualities which it had gained during this period. Nor must we imagine that the result of this work was confined to the quiet libraries and writing-rooms of the monasteries. Alfred's policy of insisting that the sons of all free men should, if their father's means allowed, receive an education in English, could not have been without its effect. The written

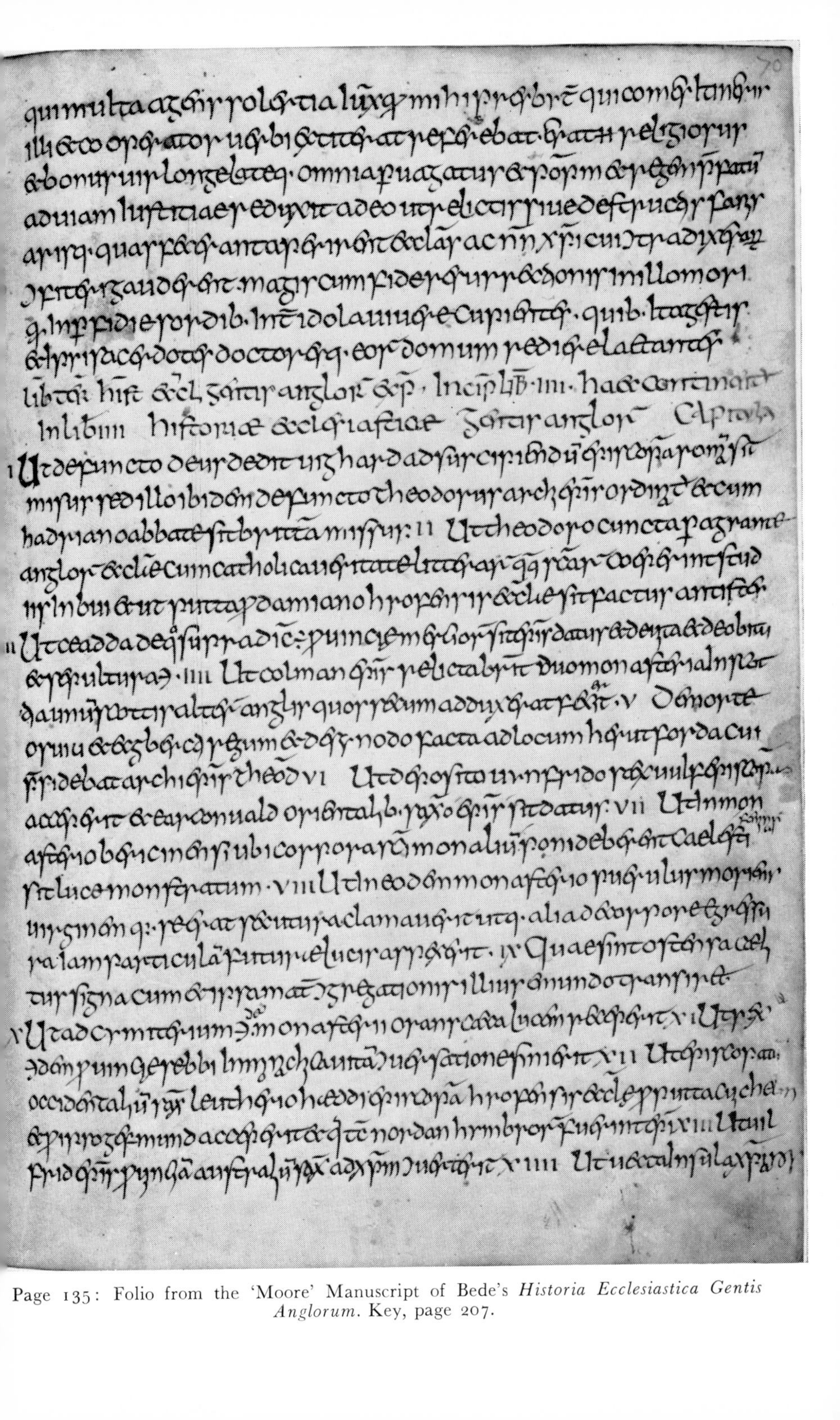

Page 135: Folio from the 'Moore' Manuscript of Bede's *Historia Ecclesiastica Gentis Anglorum*. Key, page 207.

Page 136: Page from a late thirteenth-century manuscript of Geoffrey of Monmouth's *Historia Britonum*. Key, page 209.

word was becoming an instrument available throughout the land and a workmanlike and lucid prose style was becoming widespread. Moreover, under Alfred's guidance, the status of the English tongue was significantly improved. Where, before, the use of Latin was the mark of learning it was now recognised that the language of England was English, both for the rough-and-tumble of daily conversation, and for the writing of learned works and books of devotion.

But what chiefly concerns us is the care which Alfred took to reorganise the *Anglo-Saxon Chronicle*, and to ensure its accuracy and continuity. It took many years for Alfred to bring peace to England. The defeat and baptism of Guthrum had taken place in 878, but it was not until 886 that Alfred was able to occupy London and 'all the English folk made submission to him except those who were captive to the Danes.' By about 890, however, he was able to turn from matters of war to matters of peace and build again all that had been lost during the years of destruction and struggle.

Professor Chadwick (*Origin of the English Nation*) has suggested that there was almost certainly in existence a *Chronicle* ending in 754, which therefore was over 100 years old in Alfred's day. For the period from the coming of Augustine to 754 this *Chronicle* was probably both reliable and complete, because the art of writing was by then firmly established and events would have been recorded as they occurred. The compilers, however, must have relied for the earlier period upon oral traditions, possibly upon poems and songs and at best upon the scantiest of written records. It is clear from the entries in the *Chronicle* that, during Alfred's reign, the king himself took a close interest in the records that were being kept. The entry that we have examined for 878 dealing with the battle of Edington gives a very detailed account of events. Indeed in one passage it gives the king's daily marches. It could not have been written by a monk sitting in isolation in a monastery, briefly noting down events in the busy world outside, as news and rumour came to him. This is true of many entries for this period. In 893, for example, there is a most detailed account of Alfred's campaign against the Danes, who on this occasion had been joined by dissident elements from Northumbria and East Anglia. The campaign was a complicated one, with the fighting ranging from Exeter to London, Rochester and Shoebury, and northwards to Chester. The account could only have been compiled by someone who took part in the campaign—maybe Alfred himself.

Just as Alfred had sent copies of his translations to various centres in his dominions, so now copies of the revised *Anglo-Saxon Chronicle* were sent to Winchester, Canterbury, Abingdon, Worcester, Peterborough and other monasteries. There seems little doubt that the copies circulated were of a revision of the earlier *Chronicle* brought up to date. It was at this point that the brief records dealing with the coming of the first English in the days of Vortigern were combined with the works of Bede, of whom Alfred was such an admirer. This accounts for some of the similarities between the early entries of the *Chronicle* and Bede's *History*.

Many of these manuscripts, or copies of them, still survive. At Corpus Christi College, Cambridge, is the famous Parker manuscript, so called because it once belonged to Archbishop Parker who left it to the College. This originally belonged to the monks of Winchester and later (probably just before the Norman Conquest) was sent to Canterbury. The entries up to 891 are in one hand, which provides good evidence that the *Chronicle* had been revised and edited in 891, and a completely new version made. This first scribe, although he finished his work in 891, had written the year 892 in the margin. The clerk who continued the work made further entries for the year 891, but forgot to delete the 892 in the margin. This led to some confusion, and for thirty years the entries are one year out.

In the British Museum are two eleventh-century copies of the *Chronicle* maintained at Abingdon (Manuscripts B and C). Manuscript B seems to have been made for Canterbury, and no further entries were added there. Manuscript C, however, was continued right down to 1066.

From Worcester comes Manuscript D, also in the British Museum. It was made in about 1050 and maintained at Worcester up to 1079. The original from which it was copied (now lost) was compiled in the north, probably at Ripon, the starting point having been one of the versions sent there by Alfred.

In the Bodleian Library at Oxford is Manuscript E which was maintained at Peterborough. The copy seems to have been made as late as 1121 (up to which date all the entries are in one hand) and it was continued until 1154.

As will be seen, the *Anglo-Saxon Chronicle* is not a single work but a collection of many records, maintained by many men during many ages and at many different places. Alfred left upon it the permanent impress of his scholarship and organising ability. By causing a complete edition—based upon older work—to be made, and by issuing copies to the different centres, he ensured that a coherent and orderly record of English affairs was kept until well after the Norman Conquest. Moreover, the lodging of copies in different monasteries ensured that local knowledge was brought to bear, and that more vivid and complete records were maintained than would have been possible had one single record been kept. From the time of Alfred, then, the *Chronicle* furnishes a clear account of all the chief events in England, and we no longer have to rely upon the colourful exaggerations of legend. Time and again, campaigns are described with the kind of detail that would have been available only to an eyewitness, or to men who had been closely associated with command of the armies. We are told, for example, that in 923 the English army went to Nottingham, built a fortification on the south bank of the river opposite the one on the north bank, and connected the two by means of a bridge across the Trent; the king then went to Bakewell in Derbyshire and had a fortress built there.

Not surprisingly, now that the *Chronicle* had become formalised, it began to acquire a self-consciously literary flavour. In

937, for example, a battle fought at Brunnanburgh by King Athelstan and the West Saxon army against a combined force of Norsemen and Scots is described in a long and stirring poem. (The example was followed, somewhat unsuccessfully, in 942 and again in 959 when two briefer inferior poems are inserted.)

The writing sometimes took on a political flavour and clerks, no longer content merely to record, would criticise. In 999:

> the Danes came round into the Thames and up along the Medway to Rochester. And the Kentish army came against them and they fought strongly. But they all too quickly turned and fled because they did not have the support they should have had . . . Then the king with his council ordered that the enemy should be met by a sea force and a land force. But when the ships were ready there was delay from day to day and the crews in the ships were put out by this . . . And in the end neither the ships nor the land army came to anything except labour for the people and money wasted and encouragement for the enemy.

All this happened in the unhappy reign of Aethelred ('Ethelred the Unready') and again, in 1010, the Danes came raiding. They burned Cambridge, invaded Oxfordshire and took Bedford.

> And when the enemy was in the east, our army were gathered in the west, and when they were in the south, our army was in the north. Then the council was summoned to the king because a plan for defending the kingdom had to be made at once. Whatever action was decided upon it was not followed for a single month.

We have come a long way from the brief records of the early *Chronicle*—'765: in this year Alhred succeeded to the kingdom of Northumbria and reigned eight years.' The *Chronicle* had become a sophisticated and complex document—recording, commenting upon and criticising the events of each year, the writers mourning the tragedies and acclaiming the triumphs of different ages. In fact, as reorganised and reshaped by Alfred, it provides almost the same kind of evidence that would be found in a file of newspapers; there are good contemporary accounts of the most important events, thumbnail sketches of the eminent, the occasional literary feature in the form of a poem, together with informed comment on national policy. Sometimes the entries resemble articles from a war correspondent; certainly some, like the following for 915, were drafted or dictated by men who were with the armies on campaign:

> 915. In this year Warwick was fortified and a large naval force came hither from the south from Brittany under two jarls Ohtor and Hraold [*sic*] and sailed west until they reached the Severn estuary, and harried Wales at will everywhere along its banks. They captured Cyfeilog, bishop of Archenfield and took him with them to the ships, but King Edward ransomed him afterwards for forty pounds. Then after this the whole Danish host went inland in order to renew their raids towards Archenfield. They were fought by men from Hereford and Gloucester and from the nearest boroughs who fought against them and put them to flight. They slew jarl Hraold and the other jarl Ohtor's brother and a great part of the host, and drove them into their camp and beset them until they gave them hostages and promised to depart from the king's realm. The king had ordered that the coast should be guarded against them along the south shore of the Severn estuary, from Cornwall in the west eastwards as far as the mouth of the Avon, so that they did not dare land anywhere in that region. However, they landed secretly by night twice, once east of Watchet and again at Porlock, and on each occasion the English fought them so that only a few escaped who were able to swim to the ships. They encamped on the island of Steepholme until the time came that they were short of food and many died of hunger, since they were unable to obtain supplies. Then they went from there to Dyfed and from there to Ireland. This was in the autumn. Afterwards, before Martinmas in the same year, King Edward went with his army to Buckingham and stayed there for four weeks, building both the strong points on each bank of the river before he left. Jarl Thurcytel yielded to him with all the jarls and the important men who came under Bedford and many of those who came under Northampton.

Then, in 1003, we have an acid comment upon Ealdorman Aelfric. It was his duty to take command of an army which had been raised in Wiltshire and Hampshire and to lead them against the Danes.

> But as soon as the two opposing armies came within sight of one another, Aelfric pretended to be unwell, and tried very hard to be sick, and said that he was ill, thus playing false to the men he was supposed to lead.

A fully detailed record is thus available for all that happened in England (and for some of the major events overseas) down to the time of the Norman Conquest and beyond. Thanks to the *Chronicle*, the history of England for 500 of its most vital and formative years—from the seventh to the twelfth century—is among the best-documented of any in the world. We owe much to those early clerks who, very soon after the art of writing came to England with Christianity in the early seventh century, wrote down the ancient traditions of their ancestors, and began the careful and painstaking maintenance of an annual record. And we owe much to King Alfred, defender of England and preserver of the English nation, who used the years of peace to spread learning, bring the English language into flower, and build a sound administrative framework within which the *Anglo-Saxon Chronicle* was perfected and for so long maintained.

VII

BISHOP ASSER'S LIFE OF KING ALFRED

KING ALFRED did not work single-handed. To command his armies he appointed ealdormen, as had his predecessors. To represent his person and authority in distant parts of his kingdom he appointed reeves. The sheriffs of today inherit their title from the shire-reeves of the Saxon kings, men who wielded the power of the king in the shires. Alfred also selected the bishops and appointed at least one scholar to assist him in his task of promoting learning throughout his kingdom.

For the year 910 (some nine years after King Alfred's death) the *Anglo-Saxon Chronicle* reports:

> In this year Frithustan succeeded to the bishopric of Winchester and Asser, Bishop of Sherborne died thereafter. In the same year King Edward sent armies from both Wessex and Mercia and attacked the [Danish] host in the north, destroying the folk and cattle of every sort. They killed many Danes and remained in that region for five weeks.

The times were still troubled, and King Edward, Alfred's son, was continuing the work of his father. He was organising the defence of the whole of England, raising armies not only in his own kingdom of Wessex, but in Mercia too, and sending them on a swift and merciless campaign against the Danes.

If news of the expedition came to the Bishop of Sherborne

during the months when his life was ending, he would have found the perils familiar and the victory not unexpected. For he had spent many years in the service of King Alfred, helping him in his labours of translation and composition. He had seen the fortunes of King Alfred ebb and come flooding back to his final triumph over Guthrum. Alfred himself recorded his debt to Asser. In his letter to all the bishops in England, which he sent with his translation of Gregory's *Cura Pastoralis*, Alfred wrote:

> I began . . . to turn into English the book which is named in Latin *Pastoralis* and in English *The Herdsman's Book*, whiles word by word, whiles meaning by meaning, just as I had learned from Plegmund my Archbishop, and from Asser my Bishop, and from John my mass-priest. After I had learned it, so that I could understand it, as best I could understand it, and as I could most clearly reckon it, I turned it into English.

The passage suggests that Asser was not merely an assistant to the king in his literary work, but that on occasion he also acted as the king's tutor. Now, in his old age, Bishop Asser would have been proud that Alfred's son was stoutly resisting the Danish invaders and that English arms were again victorious.

The years following Alfred's death had been full of difficulty. Edward, the new king, had had to contend not only with the Danes but with his own cousin Aethelwold. The latter, in the very year that Alfred died, seized the manor of Wimborne without the consent of the king and his council. King Edward rode with his soldiers to Wimborne and Aethelwold, with the men who had sworn to support him, barricaded himself within the manor and swore that he would stay, dead or alive. Then in the dark of night he slipped out of the house, evaded the king's men, and rode north to join the Danish host in Northumbria. The only satisfaction which the king had was that he rescued a nun whom Aethelwold had snatched from a convent in defiance of sanctity and the orders of the bishop.

Aethelwold appears to have gone abroad, for three years later the *Anglo-Saxon Chronicle* mentions his coming 'here from overseas to Essex with the ships that came with him'. In the following year Aethelwold persuaded the Danes in East Anglia to declare war against the English. They harried acrossed Mercia until they crossed the Thames at Cricklade. King Edward, as soon as he could raise his armies, drove them back into East Anglia. There a detachment of the men of Kent who had marched with King Edward were set upon by the Danes. In the fighting there was great slaughter and two ealdormen were killed on the English side, as well as one of the king's thanes and a bishop. The Danish King Beohtric was killed, and so was Aethelwold—who had urged him on to this fatal war. In the following year King Edward made peace with the Danes and the Northumbrians. The first five years of Edward's reign, then, were occupied in what was at that time the royal business of raising armies from the farms and cottages of the realm, and spending long days in the saddle in pursuit of those who sought the destruction of his kingdom.

Four years later, after the battle in East Anglia, fighting between the Danes and the English was resumed, and in the same year (910) Bishop Asser died.

It was during these troubled years that Bishop Asser, as an act of pious duty and perhaps of friendship, wrote the life of his royal master and patron, King Alfred the Great. His work, in Latin, is entitled *Annales Rerum Gestarum Aelfredi Magni* (*Annals of the Deeds of Alfred the Great*). No ancient manuscript has survived. The one copy of the work, probably made during the eleventh century, formed part of the great collection made by Sir Robert Coxson. In 1731 Sir Robert's house in Westminster caught fire, and the Asser manuscript was totally destroyed. We have, therefore, to rely upon secondary sources. Fortunately, Sir Francis Wise had made an excellent copy just before the fire, thereby saving Asser's book for posterity. The best transcript is today at Corpus Christi College, Cambridge.

Scholars have for long disputed whether the biography of

Alfred is indeed the work of Asser, or whether it was written 150 years later and ascribed to the good Bishop of Sherborne in order to gain credibility. Certainly there would have been every temptation to do so, for anyone who wished to claim contemporary authenticity for a later work. Asser's existence had been firmly proved by the entry in the *Anglo-Saxon Chronicle* for 910 and in Alfred's own letter—from both of which we have already quoted. Moreover there are some errors and inconsistencies in the book, as we shall see, which make it difficult to accept certain passages as having been written by a well-informed intimate of the king. On the other hand these passages may well be additions by later copyists, and in this context we must remember that the lost manuscript, from which all our existing versions derive, may well have contained many interpolations. As P. J. Helm wrote 'In the absence of final proof it is safer to accept his [Asser's] account, but to bear in mind that the text has almost certainly been tampered with'.

Asser tells us that Alfred, King of the Anglo-Saxons, was born in 849 in the village of 'Wanating in the district which is called Berrocsire'. This is Wantage, in Berkshire, where a statue of Alfred was placed in the market place during the reign of Queen Victoria. His mother was Osburga, an extremely religious woman and daughter of Oslac, King Aethelwulf's steward. Oslac himself is described as descended from the Goths and Jutes so that, according to Asser, Alfred was of mixed descent. On his father's side Asser traces his descent back to Cerdic, the first king of the West Saxons, who came to Britain in 495. After the death of Osburga, Alfred's father Aethelwulf married Judith, a daughter of Charles, King of the Franks.

The book starts by giving an account of affairs in Wessex, and closely follows the *Anglo-Saxon Chronicle*. The link between the narrative and Alfred's life is quite tenuous. Asser simply relates the date of each main event with Alfred's age at the time:

In the year of our Lord's incarnation 860 which was the twelfth year of King Alfred's age, Aethelbald King of the West Saxons died . . .

> In the year of our Lord's incarnation 866 which was the eighteenth year of King Alfred's age, Aethelred who was the brother of Aethelbert, King of the West Saxons, took over the kingdom for five years . . .

This is not biography. But it is evidence—albeit slight—for Asser's authorship. He did not meet Alfred until the king was about thirty-six years old, and it is to be expected that, apart from one or two outstanding incidents which Alfred himself might have remembered and told him, Asser's account of Alfred's childhood would have been brief.

One of the events in Alfred's childhood which Asser describes was a memory which Alfred himself treasured throughout his life and shared with his tutor. It is the kind of story which he would have recalled when he was working on some literary project with Bishop Asser, the work reminding him of the days when he first became the owner of a book.

> One day, his mother showed him and his brother a certain book of English poetry which she had in her hand. 'Whichever one of you,' she said, 'is most quickly able to learn this book, I'll give it to him.' Stimulated by what she had said (or rather by divine inspiration) and delighted by the beautiful capital letter in the book, and answering his mother before all his brothers who, although senior in age were not so in grace, he said 'Will you really give that book to one of us, that is to say the one who can quickest understand it and recite it to you?' At this she smiled and was very pleased and said 'Of course I will give it!' Then he straight away took the book out of her hand and went to his master to read it. And when he had read it, brought it back to his mother and recited it.

Afterwards he learned the church services and the psalms and many prayers, which were in a book which he kept with him night and day— 'As I myself have seen' says Asser. Alfred unhappily could not have a liberal education because there were no good readers in the whole West Saxon kingdom. Alfred himself recalls this in the letter he wrote accompanying his translation of Pope Gregory's *Cura Pastoralis.*

Asser describes in detail the terrible events of 871 when Alfred was twenty-three and acting as second-in-command to his brother King Aethelred. The Danes were triumphant and the two brothers had suffered a defeat at Reading. Four days later they fought the heathen army at Aescesdun (today's Ashdown on the Berkshire Downs). Asser describes the engagement in detail. The Danes occupied the higher ground so that the English had to attack uphill. Alfred led his men forward without waiting for his brother, who was praying. The two armies met near a stunted thorn tree— 'Which I myself have never seen'. (The name of the Hundred hereabouts is given in Domesday Book as *Nachedethorn*—Naked Thorn.) Asser records that one Danish King (the *Anglo-Saxon Chronicle* says two), five Earls and many thousands of men died that day, and that their corpses covered the whole breadth of Ashdown.

Later that year King Aethelred died and Alfred became king. His brother had left two young sons, but this was no time for a child to wield the sword of Wessex.

The account given by Asser of Alfred's campaigns adds little to what we already know from the *Anglo-Saxon Chronicle*. He tells one story of Alfred's adventures, though, which is not to be found elsewhere. When Alfred was in hiding in Somerset, his army reduced to a small troop of faithful followers and his kingdom shrunk to the marshlands around Athelney, he was sitting by the fire in the house of a herdsman who had given him shelter. He was adjusting his bow, preparing his arrows and other gear while the herdsman's wife was baking bread. She relied upon the stranger by the hearth to watch the baking, and was horrified to see that, engrossed in working on his weapons, he had let the loaves burn. 'You'll eat them fast enough when they are done,' she said angrily; 'couldn't you have looked after them a little better?'

This story, which has become embedded in England's folklore, is certainly not part of Asser's original work. It was first printed in 1574 in Archbishop Parker's edition of Asser's book, and first appears in a twelfth-century account of St Neot, a Cornish saint. The loaves are not burnt, but the herdsman's wife rebukes Alfred for not being quicker in turning them. The passage dealing with this incident refers to the *Life of St Neot*, and this alone proves it to be an interpolation since St Neot lived in the tenth century, 100 years and more after Asser's death.

When Alfred started trying to re-establish learning throughout his kingdom, he sent for the Welsh monk Asser, whose reputation must have stood high. 'He received me kindly,' wrote Asser, 'and among other intimate matters, warmly invited me to enter his service and to become his friend.' Asser was cautious, and although the king promised to make good any possessions which Asser might have left in Wales, the most he would promise was that he would spend six months of each year with the king and six months in Wales.

In fact, after returning home for a brief period, Asser spent eight months with the king. During this time he read aloud to the king, for Alfred was accustomed

> by day and by night, among all his preoccupations of mind and of body, to read books himself or to listen while others read aloud to him.

At dusk on Christmas Eve he sent for Asser and gave him two monasteries. As if even this princely gift was not enough, he gave him a precious silk vestment and a great quantity of incense—as much as a man could carry. Later he was to give him many other costly gifts.

This seems genuine enough. But there follows another interpolated passage purporting to give an account of a dispute between Grimbold (a French scholar who was visiting Oxford) and 'the old scholars whom he had found there', who are supposed to have been anxious to prove to Grimbold that Oxford had been a centre of learning long before he came to visit them. They advanced as evidence the fact that both Gildas and Nennius had once studied there—a claim which, if true, would make Oxford a very ancient university indeed. If the interpolator is truly recording (which is improbable) a dispute between Grimbold and the Oxford dons, then certainly the views of Grimbold are more likely to be true, since there is no evidence for Oxford as a centre of learning in the days of Gildas and Nennius.

After this most dubious passage, the main narrative is resumed with an account of events in 887, when Alfred was thirty-nine, and Asser had served his royal master for some three years. We are told of the Danish fleet sailing up the River Seine 'under the bridge' and so to the Marne. We are given an account of the death of King Charles of the Franks, and how five kings were appointed to succeed him, with Arwulf his nephew chief among them.

Far more interesting is Asser's story of how, in that same year, Alfred started his studies in earnest and began to fit himself for his tasks of translation.

> One day we were both sitting in the king's room, chatting as usual about various topics, and I by chance read a passage to him out of a book. He was all ears, and listened carefully. Then he spoke to me thoughtfully and at the same time showed me a book which he had about him. In this, the daily services, and the prayers and psalms, which he had read as a young man were all written down. He asked me to write in it the passage I had read.

Asser conceived the idea of using this incident to prompt Alfred to start a second book in which further Latin quotations might be copied. He asked the king whether he might write the quotation on a separate sheet. Alfred agreed and on the same day Asser found three other quotations which the king liked. Thereafter they talked together every day and Asser continually found further quotations, so that the sheet was soon full. From the first, Alfred was anxious to read the various passages and to translate them into English. The single sheet rapidly grew into a book, which King Alfred called his *Enchirdion* or 'Handbook'. In the end the book grew to the size of a psalter. It is extraordinary that Alfred came to his serious studies so late in life. Asser likens him in this regard to the repentant thief who turned to the truth at the very end. The next passage describes King Alfred's many tribulations, including ill health:

> For, from the time that he was twenty until now, when he is forty, he has suffered continual and severe attacks from an obscure illness, so that he has not had a moment's relief, either from the pain caused by the illness, nor from the depression from which he suffers in anticipation of an attack.

This passage presents considerable difficulty. It was written some time in 887, one year after Asser had initiated the king's 'Handbook', and clearly Alfred was alive at the time ('until now, when he is forty'). The book could not, in one brief year, have grown to the length of the psalter; the king had a kingdom to govern, and had to pursue his scholarship in odd moments. Is the contradiction between the two passages due to the clumsiness of a careless forger, fabricating a work and falsely ascribing it to Asser? Liars must have good memories, it is said, and it is almost inconceivable that a forger would so blatantly contradict himself from one page to another. A likelier explanation is that Asser made notes from time to time of his conversations with the king, and that this passage represents such a note, transcribed in full into the main work at a later date. Certainly it has all the marks of a contemporary account.

King Alfred's ill health is mentioned more than once. In an earlier chapter, dealing with the king's marriage, we are told that he was seized with a sudden severe pain during the celebrations. This painful malady stayed with him 'from his twentieth to his fortieth year, and even longer than that . . .' (which shows that Asser's work was written *after* the king's fortieth year). This sudden illness was not his first. He had suffered pain since childhood and as a young man had prayed that God might relieve him of his sickness, giving him instead some lighter and less painful affliction—but, not one that disfigured him physically. 'For,' wrote Asser, 'he had a great fear of leprosy and blindness.' So the picture is of a man who suffered continuous pain and who was, perhaps, somewhat sickly in his youth. All of which makes the vigour and resolution of Alfred's campaigns, and the immense labours of his peacetime tasks, the more remarkable.

He certainly did not spare himself. Asser, after describing the illness, reminds us that Alfred was continually harassed by the invasions of the Danes. He built or restored many fortified towns, dealt with foreign ambassadors and had to endure quarrels and arguments among his friends and advisers. He personally gave orders to his bishops, military commanders, ministers and representatives. Sometimes he had to exhort them, sometimes rebuke them. A long passage describes his difficulties with his subordinates, his reproofs, and his occasional impatience.

In an attempt to re-establish the monasteries, which had been almost destroyed during the Danish invasions, Alfred invited from abroad learned men and children so that the cloisters might be peopled again and the work of scholarship restored. Even here he had his problems. Two French monks, jealous of their Abbot, conspired to murder him. It was their intention to leave his body by the door of a well-known whore, so that it might appear that the Abbot had been slain when visiting her, thus bringing disrepute upon his name and the entire monastery. The plot failed and the villains were arrested and put to death.

No man could lead such a full life without a high degree of organisation; Alfred organised both his income and his time efficiently. He resolved, Asser tells us, to devote half his hours, both by day and by night, to the service of God; and in the same way to devote one half of his revenues to the same purpose. One-third of the part assigned to worldly uses went to his scholars, his ministers, and the nobles who attended upon him. (The cost of running the kingdom fell in those days directly upon the king.) One-third went to the artisans and builders who worked on the various construction projects he had organised; and one-third was paid to visitors from overseas.

The second portion, to be devoted to God's service, was divided into five parts: one was given to the poor, one went to the two monasteries he had founded, one to the school he had established and one to all the monasteries in Wessex and Mercia. In some years, part of this last portion went to the churches and clergy in Gaul, Brittany, Wales, Cornwall and Northumberland.

So that his time might be divided with equal precision, he had candles made of standard size and weight and marked at intervals, accurately showing the passing of the hours.

His conception of kingship was an interesting one. He did not identify himself with the aristocracy. He devoted a great deal of attention to the poor and was their constant protector. He was himself the kingdom's court of appeal, and anyone who felt aggrieved by a judgement in the courts could go before him. He was a careful and thorough investigator, probing deeply, so that men did not lightly appear before him. Nor did he wait for appeals to be made, but studied almost all the judgements made in the kingdom, and would call the attention of the judges to any apparent injustice. His commanders and officers would tremble at the rebukes which he administered; he did not spare subordinates when he felt they had fallen short of his high standards.

Asser ends his book with an engaging description of some of Alfred's elderly officers, who had lacked all formal education when young, laboriously studying the liberal arts. Many of them, who could not read, had their sons or a servant read to them.

The Life of King Alfred is a precious and fascinating document which gives an intimate contemporary picture of King Alfred—stern, tireless, a friend of the poor, full of nervous energy in spite of nagging pain and ill-health, insisting upon high standards of learning in his officers, and himself carefully studying every detail of affairs. In addition to the portrait of the king, it shows something of the way in which kingship was organised among the early English. Perhaps it was pride that prompted Asser to write his book, in order to show himself as an intimate friend of a great king. If so, pride can rarely have borne better fruit.

VIII

WILLIAM OF MALMESBURY

ABOUT 160 years after the death of Alfred, who had demonstrated the stubbornness and resilience of the English, the army of England was decisively beaten by an invader in one single engagement. Not since the swift campaign by the legions of Claudius, over 1,000 years before, had power in the island changed hands so swiftly. The forces of the stern Duke of Normandy, consisting of his own feudal levies reinforced by ruthless adventurers from Brittany, Flanders and other parts of France, gained possession of the kingdom in one day's desperate fighting near Hastings.

To the English, and particularly to those aware of the island's history, the drama of Hastings must have been startling. Their ancestors had had to fight their way into Britain in a long series of bloody battles extending over nearly two centuries. The Danes had raided, harried and wasted the land for even longer, and however often their hosts had scattered the armies of the English, other English armies had gathered and fought back with a persistence that survived all defeats. But now the English, more resolute than the Britons, as grim and battle-eager as the Danes, had been shattered in one September afternoon. With the stubborn but defeated troops who died at Hastings, among whose bruised and bleeding corpses lay the body of their king, Harold Godwinson, there had died a whole era. A foreign king now wielded the sceptre of Wessex and of England; for centuries the English language was to be banished from court and council. English thanes were to be dispossessed of the lands which they and their forefathers had held proudly for generations and their cornlands and pastures given as rewards to the adventurers who had assisted in the work of conquest. Free Englishmen were to see the grey castles of their oppressors built throughout the land.

How had this come about? Harold's army had fought bravely and had shown the same spirit as had the armies of Alfred. The English soldiers had refused to acknowledge defeat and had died where they stood. But that autumn, England had been beset by two enemies at once.

Just before the Norman invasion, news came to King Harold that the King of Norway had landed with an army in the north. Harold led his troops by forced marches to face this new danger and fought two battles in the space of five weary days. His victorious but exhausted men, their numbers reduced by the casualties they had suffered, then set out on the long march from York to the south coast, as news came that William of Normandy had landed his invasion force at Pevensey. These were the men who, in a few desperate days, had marched along the old Roman road from London to York, had taken part in two hard-fought actions, had marched back to London and beyond, and now faced a new enemy. The overwhelming defeat suffered by the English at Sandlake, near Hastings, was therefore no disgrace. Neither Harold nor his men had failed in courage or in duty; even in defeat they had done nothing to make any man ashamed of being English.

Indeed, soon after the Norman Conquest came a revival of interest in the origins and past achievements of the English nation. It began to be realised by Norman and Englishman alike that the laws, traditions, and institutions developed over 500 years were more powerful than the innovations brought by the Normans, and were worthy of study and preservation.

The *Anglo-Saxon Chronicle* was being maintained in the

monastery of Peterborough, so that the raw material of history was still being carefully stored away. What was new was an interest not merely in continuing these records, but in studying and interpreting past documents. Bede had done just this three centuries earlier, but his example had not been widely followed. True, some seventy years before the Norman Conquest a member of the royal family, Aethelweard, had written in Latin *A Chronicle from the Beginning of the World to the Year of Our Lord 972*. His stated purpose was to record the deeds of his ancestors 'as far as my memory will help, and according to what my parents taught me'. He addressed his book to his kinswoman Matilda, a descendant of King Alfred. His grandfather was probably related to Ealdorman Brihtnoth, whose gallant stand against the Danes at Maldon, where he died in the fighting, was one of the few memorable episodes of the disastrous reign of Aethelred 'the Unready'. Aethelweard was a great-grandson of that other King Aethelred, Alfred's brother and predecessor. Unfortunately his work is not as distinguished as his ancestry. Having summarised the story of Vortigern, he translated into Latin the *Anglo-Saxon Chronicle*, adding very little new material. His Latin was poor, his chronology confused, and his transcription of proper names careless.

Perhaps the greatest of those who wrote in the years immediately after the Norman Conquest was William, a monk of Malmesbury. Like Bede, of whom he was a great admirer, he had been placed in a monastery as a boy. He thus grew up in an atmosphere of learning and scholarship, becoming librarian and also precentor. Devoting his life to study, he declined the office of Abbot which was later offered to him. He was probably born some thirty years after the Battle of Hastings, when the bitterness of the conquest had faded. He died some time after 1142, which is the last year covered by one of his historical works. He himself tells us that he was of mixed English and Norman descent and he was therefore typical of the new generation that was growing up among the wealthy classes in England. He was a prolific writer; some nineteen works can confidently be ascribed to him.

The most important of his books is *De Gestis Regum Anglorum* (*The History of the Kings of England*). In its preface he wrote:

> The history of the English people, from their coming into Britain until his own times, was written by Bede—a man of outstanding learning and modesty—in a lucid and engaging style. In my opinion, you will not easily find any others who, after him, have attempted to write a history of this nation in Latin.

He then lists the material which was available to him, beginning with the *Anglo-Saxon Chronicle*, which he refers to as 'notes about ancient times, written in the style of a chronicle, in the English language'. He rightly states that it is due entirely to the *Chronicle* that any record of events after the death of Bede had been preserved. He adds

> About Elward [Aethelweard], an eminent nobleman who tried to translate that chronicle into Latin, and whose intention I could more easily praise if his language did not displease me, it is better to be silent.

He also mentions a work by Eadmer, a monk from Canterbury, who wrote *Historia Novorum* (*A History of Modern Times*), covering the years 1066 to 1122.

It was the poorly documented period after the death of Bede that William made his especial interest. He pointed out that there was, as it were, a gap in the recorded history of England and added

> This circumstance has prompted me (both out of love for my country as well as out of respect for the authority of those who have instructed me to take up this work) to fill the gap and to work up the rough material with the art of the Romans.

William was certainly making no idle boast. His skill in 'the art of the Romans' was great, his style polished, and his tastes classical. He quotes Virgil in his preface and there are many classical allusions throughout the work.

Unfortunately his references to his sources are limited to English books, and he does not say from which British authorities he drew his account of the first coming of the English, and of their fierce struggle with the Britons. It is clear, from the very beginning of his book, that he made very careful use of the earlier writers to whom he referred, and that he was a man of real scholarship. Where he records matters that are not to be found in any of his known sources, we may believe what he tells us, and assume that he is working from other unknown material which he considered to be reliable.

Book I opens with the arrival of the Angles and Saxons who, it is said, came into Britain in the year 449. This is evidently taken from the *Anglo-Saxon Chronicle*. William is wrong in ascribing the arrival of Hengist's men to that particular year. The *Chronicle* merely uses this date to mark the opening of the reign of 'Mauricius' (only the Laud manuscript correctly gives the name of Marcian) and Valentinian, adding that 'it was during their time' that the troops from Germany were invited by Vortigern.

Britain, writes William, was considered by the Romans to be an important province, as is evidenced not merely by their own writings, but by the ruins of their ancient buildings which were still to be seen throughout England. He reminds us that many of their emperors, 'rulers of almost the whole world', visited the island and spent their days there. Two, Severus and Constantius Chlorus, died and were buried in Britain. He also tells us that Constantius left a son, Constantine, who used the army of Britain to further his ambitions on the Continent and who, with the help of that army, reached the very summit of power and became sole ruler of the world. He adds that Constantine settled the veterans of the army of Britain on the western coast of Gaul, thus explaining the origin of Brittany. We do not know how true this is; other traditions ascribe the foundations of Brittany to the banishment there of the soldiers of Maximus, some seventy years after Constantine, who also took the legions of Britain across to the Continent, to enjoy a brief triumph and to suffer ultimate defeat.

William gives an acount of Maximus and of the last emperor to be appointed in Britain; this was a private soldier, of no ability or distinction, who was acclaimed as emperor for no better reason than that his name was Constantine.

So William moves to the days of Vortigern, and gives an account that seems to be drawn very largely from the works of Gildas. He enlarges upon the latter's criticisms of the actions of Vortigern, whom he describes as

> a man fit neither for the battlefield nor the council chamber, but given up entirely to the sins of the flesh and a captive of every single vice. He was a man of insatiable avarice, abundant pride, and corrupted by his own lusts.

He omits Gildas's account of the last desperate appeal of the beleaguered Britons to the Consul Aetius. However, where Gildas tells us simply that Vortigern and his counsellors invited 'the savage and unholy Saxons, a nation hateful both to God and men, to resist the invasion of the northern tribes', William explains the reasons that lay behind the decision:

> For it was considered, because of their skill in war, that these nations would easily conquer their enemies. And, as they had no lands of their own, they would gladly accept even poor lands, provided that they were given permanent homes in which to live. What is more, they could not be suspected of entering into any plot against the Britons, since gratitude for the kindness shown to them would mitigate their natural ferocity.

This is probably no more than the sensible comment of a careful historian, and we must not assume that it is necessarily based upon any contemporary records. Nevertheless it is interesting to note that William the Englishman is far more sympathetic and balanced in his assessment of Vortigern's action than Gildas the Briton. We must not totally exclude the possibility that William was using a lost British source, containing a full account of the deliberations of the Britons and the considerations that moved them. For, as we shall see, he seems to have had access to tradition or documents of the Britons other than the works of Gildas and Nennius. He adds details of how ambassadors were chosen to visit Germany to invite the tribes to Britain, and then gives the story, which Nennius also records, of Vortigern's marriage to Hengist's daughter, and of how Hengist was then given the kingdom of Kent.

For the final break between Vortigern and Hengist and for the events which next followed, William appears to have turned to the *Anglo-Saxon Chronicle*. He describes how Hengist's men broke the treaty, and the passage seems to be drawn from the entry in the *Chronicle* for 455. According to William, there followed several minor battles and four major engagements, and here again he is following the *Chronicle*. But immediately afterwards, he appears to be making use of a British source which is not the work of Gildas or Nennius. Referring to the death of Vortigern's son Vortimer, he says:

> When he died the strength of the Britons diminished and all hope left them. They would soon have been altogether destroyed if Ambrosius, the sole survivor of the Romans who became king after Vortigern, had not defeated the presumptuous barbarians with the powerful aid of the warlike Arthur.

There are two significant points about this passage. First, the phrase 'presumptuous barbarians' makes it clear that William is working from a British, not an English, source. He was writing his book, as he tells us, 'out of love of my country', and would not have used such words, charged with the contempt of the Britons for the invaders of their land. Gildas himself referred to the Britons as 'the citizens', for the Britons still saw themselves as citizens of the dying Empire, and all those nations who came from beyond the Empire's frontiers were barbarians. William's phrase is thus certainly drawn from a British source, and almost certainly from a document written in the fifth or sixth centuries, after which time the conception of citizen and barbarian had begun to fade. Finally, the reference to Arthur shows that the source is not Gildas, who does not mention Arthur by name. Nor is it Nennius, for the latter does not link Arthur's name with Ambrosius.

We may therefore, speculate that William had access to a now-lost British document. If so, then this material was to some extent consistent with the account given by Gildas of the Britons flocking to Ambrosius 'like bees in a storm' after the failure of Vortigern's policy and the savage mutiny of the German troops whom he had enlisted.

A sentence in William's book suggests that he searched in vain for some hard facts about 'the warlike Arthur'; already legend and myth were exaggerating and concealing Arthur's real achievement. William was critical enough to recognise this and to see, not without exasperation, that by now most of the evidence had become fable. He writes 'It is of this Arthur that the Britons fondly tell so many fables, even to the present day.' His few words summing up Arthur are as convincing today as they were when he wrote them nearly 900 years ago: 'a man worthy to be celebrated not by idle fictions but by authentic history.' William was obviously scrutinising his material carefully, rejecting what seemed to be mere legend. Accordingly considerable weight may be given to what he says about the period of the first coming of the English and of the resistance of the Britons, even though he was writing 600 years later.

He describes the Battle of Badon as a siege—an interesting new detail. He also tells us that 900 Saxons were engaged, a credible number: the armies fighting in Britain would not have been numerous, and this seems a much more acceptable estimate than that of Nennius, who wrote that 940 of the English were slaughtered by Arthur. It seems that Nennius mistook the figure of those engaged for the casualty list, an error which William avoided. He also tells us that Arthur had with him an image of the Virgin Mary, fixed to his armour. This again indicates that he used a source independent of Nennius, who recorded that Arthur carried an image of the Virgin at his eighth battle, the Battle of Guinnion, and not at the Battle of Badon.

So William throws new light on the British victory at Badon, which can now be seen as a siege during which Arthur's forces surrounded the Saxons, probably in a fortified place. The *Welsh Annals*, it will be recalled, suggests that the battle lasted for three days and three nights, consistent with William's account of a siege. The *Annals* further tell us that Arthur carried the Cross during this engagement; though this contradicts William in detail, it confirms in general terms that Arthur carried a Christian emblem as his banner. The battle so briefly mentioned by Gildas begins to emerge from the darkness; there is Arthur, alone, with none of the armies of the Kings of Britain who had previously fought under his command, attacking and defeating a force of nearly 1,000 of his pagan enemies; there is the three-day siege, during which the Christian standard of the Britons stood menacingly among the spears which kept the Saxons in their stronghold; there is the final charge in which many Saxons died, so that for a whole generation they ceased their attacks, and the Britons turned again to peace.

The next event described by William is the feast at which Hengist caused the leaders of the Britons to be slaughtered. The first thing to be noted is that William is not giving an account of events in correct chronological order. The Battle of Badon, as we know from Gildas and from the *Welsh Annals*, was fought long after the reign of Vortigern, whereas the banquet at which the Britons were murdered, according to both Nennius and William, was attended by King Vortigern. It appears then that the Arthurian passage of William's work represents a separate document which he transcribed and inserted as a whole into his narrative, out of strict sequence. Again we seem to be near a lost chronicle of Arthur—as we were when considering the works of Nennius—of which this passage may represent a fragment. It appears to begin after William's account of the four pitched battles between the Britons and the English, at the point where he describes how Vortimer, a son of Vortigern, died and how thereafter the British strength decayed.

Turning to William's account of the feast where Vortigern's men were slaughtered, we again find that he is not following the account given by Nennius. There is no mention of the pre-arranged signal given by Hengist for his men to fall upon the unsuspecting Britons and butcher them. It is possible that William has edited Nennius's account, removing those parts which imply that his Saxon forbears were treacherous and cold-blooded murderers. Yet the treachery is still there, though it takes a different form. In William's account Hengist invited Vortigern and 300 of his companions (the same number as that given by Nennius) to a banquet. He gave them more to drink than was usual and by taunts and mockery deliberately incited them to a quarrel in which all were killed.

After this passage, and after the death of Hengist, there follows a summary history of the kingdoms of Kent. This, the first English kingdom to be established in Britain, achieved no lasting military greatness. Within a few generations it occupied a position of secondary importance, being often dependent upon the West Saxons and Mercia, and frequently conquered by them. William's account is as brief as Kent's glory. He is content with a reference to Hengist's son Eisc (the Aesc of the *Anglo-Saxon Chronicle*) and grandson Eormanric. He gives no account of either's reign, leaving unchronicled the events of a century. He moves straight to the reign of Aethilberht, son of Eormanric, and to the coming of St Augustine. It is clear that for William, although he had carefully cut a path through the tangle of earlier events, the true history of England really began with the conversion of the English by Augustine.

William's history of Kent is based on the works of Bede and on the *Anglo-Saxon Chronicle* and adds little to what we already knew. There are however some new details. For example, where the *Anglo-Saxon Chronicle* merely says that Mul (the brother of King Caedwalla of Wessex) was burned, William tells us how it happened. The men of Kent had driven Mul into a little house which they surrounded and set on fire. Mul perished in the flames.

The second chapter of Book I is concerned with the kings of the West Saxons—the proud and warlike descendants of Cerdic. Again he largely follows the account given by the *Anglo-Saxon Chronicle* to which he frequently refers. He takes the curt entries of the *Chronicle* and rewrites them into a coherent and organised history. He more than fulfills the promise in his preface to decorate the raw material with Roman skill. For example, in recounting the attempt by the king of Wessex to have Edwin of Northumbria assassinated by an agent, he makes an apposite quotation from Virgil's *Aeneid*.

This section contains one lengthy passage of very great importance. Having brought the story of Wessex down to the days of King Cenwalh, who succeeded to the kingdom in 643, William breaks off his narrative and writes

> Since we have reached the times of Cenwalh, and since this is the proper place for referring to the monastery of Glastonbury, I shall write an account of the foundation and advancement of that church, from its very origin, in so far as I can discover it from all the evidence available.

William then tells the story, which we have already noted in Bede, of the mission sent by Pope Eleutherius to the Britons at the request of King Lucius. This was supposed by Bede to have happened in the days of Emperor Marcus Antoninus Verus who came to power in Rome in AD 156. William tells us that it was the men of this mission, 'whose names have been erased by the rust of antiquity', who built the ancient church of St Mary at Glastonbury, 'as true tradition has handed down to us through ages long past'. We know that the story of King Lucius is not true, and William's attribution of the church to these missionaries cannot be accepted. However the passage certainly attests a belief, current in William's own times, of the immense antiquity of Glastonbury. William indeed advances other evidence for this. He says that 'there are documents of good credibility, which have been found in certain places', stating that the church of St Mary was built by the hands of Christ's own Apostles.

The age in which William lived was one of credulity; nevertheless, William realised that his statement that a church in Britain had been founded by the Apostles would be met with surprise and even disbelief except in the region of Glastonbury itself, so he assures us that the tale 'is not far removed from probability'. He points to the story that Gaul had been visited by the Apostle Philip, who he suggests might well have crossed into Britain.

Leaving 'imagination and doubtful matters', William then proceeds to adduce more concrete evidence for the antiquity of Glastonbury. First he points out that it was known to the Saxons as 'the Old Church', which suggests that it was already ancient in St Augustine's day. It was built of wattle and enjoyed a very special sanctity which, as it were, spread from it over the whole country. Rich and poor alike thronged to it, and it became a centre of both religious and learned men. William offers as further evidence the story that Gildas lived there for many years. This tale, if true, would take the church back to the sixth century. In any event, says William, 'this church is surely the oldest that I know in England'. He describes the floor, 'inlaid with polished stone' and the patterns upon it, all of which is suggestive of a Roman mosiac. He also tells us of the numerous relics that were kept around the altar. The holy atmosphere surrounding the church was such that anyone who polluted it, or who brought hawk or horse within the church grounds, would suffer grievously for it. On the other hand, any man who had to undergo ordeal by fire or water, and who prayed there, would escape. He recorded that this had happened within living memory. He added the significant detail that

> men of that region swear no more frequent or holy oath than an oath by the Old Church; and they fear swift punishment if they should commit perjury in this regard.

Remembering the tales that were later written down of the preservation at Glastonbury of the Holy Grail, the special quality of the oath takes on a special interest. Oaths were customarily taken upon relics, and if among those kept at the church there was one of unique grace, then the particular quality of the oath could be explained.

William also records large numbers of documents which he refrains from quoting (lest he should weary his readers), all of which showed the great age of the place and in what veneration it was held by the local rulers. How we wish that he had been less sensitive about the fatigue of his readers, and had transcribed at least some of these documents, now lost to us!

He also mentions the existence of pyramids near the church, the tallest of which was some twenty-eight feet high, built in five sections. The topmost section contained the statue of a pope; in the next there was a statue of a king with an inscription which William gives as *Her Sexi* and *Bisperh*. He records other names from the lower sections, and then describes a second pyramid, twenty-six feet in height, with four sections; the names on this were Centwin, Bishop Hedda, Bregored and Beorward. He suggests that these pyramids were burial places, and that inside them stone coffins would be found containing the bones of the men whose names were inscribed. He tells us that Bregored and Beorward were Abbots of Glastonbury in the times of the Britons.

In the next passage William lists the abbots of Glastonbury.

There is a lengthy and important reference to St David of Menevia, who 'proved the antiquity and holiness of the church by a divine vision'. Intending to dedicate the church, he came to the place with his seven suffragan bishops. Everything was made ready for the ceremony. During the night, when he was asleep, David saw Jesus standing by him, asking gently why he had come. When David explained the reason, the Lord dissuaded him from carrying out the rites, saying that 'the Church had already been dedicated by Himself in honour of His Mother and that the ceremony was not to be profaned by human repetition.' The story is evidence of a very old belief in the antiquity of the Church, and in its having been founded if not by Christ himself then at least by his contemporaries.

Paulinus, says William, who came to Britain with St Augustine, protected the fabric of the old wattle church by placing around it a shell of new timber. When we remember the hostility that developed between the Church of the Britons and Augustine, the action of Paulinus in restoring and protecting Glastonbury is noteworthy. The church there must have possessed some very special value to prompt such action, and this fact too is indirect evidence of its antiquity and reputation.

Five years after Augustine's arrival, the British King of Devon granted to the Old Church 'the land called Ineswitrin'. William quoted a few words from the original deed of gift which he appears to have seen. The name of the bishop who wrote the deed is given as Maworn, and that of the abbot as Worgrez. In support of his belief that the document was genuine, William pointed to the word 'Ineswitrin' which is the name the Britons had for the spot—*the Isle of Glass*. He ends his account of Glastonbury, and justifies its insertion at this particular point, by referring to King Cenwalh, who made a gift of land to the abbot of two hides (possibly about 240 acres).

This is one of the earliest surviving accounts of Glastonbury and it contains much extremely useful material. For example, there is no reference to the existence of Arthur's tomb, or to any tradition that he was buried there. Had either physical traces or firm traditions existed, there can be little doubt that William would have referred to the matter. The earlier passage quoted shows how anxious he was to find any evidence that would take Arthur from the shadowy realm of fable and place him in the sunlit landscape of history.

In the same way, his silence on the story of Joseph of Arimathea must be taken as evidence against its authenticity. William, as he himself says, made use both of current legends and of old documents at Glastonbury and elsewhere. If the Joseph story be true, it is hard to believe that he found no trace of it worthy to be recorded. His account leaves the impression that the church at Glastonbury was immensely old, that there was a firm belief going back over many centuries that it was founded in apostolic times, but that the story of Joseph of Arimathea remains not proven.

Resuming the story of Wessex, he again follows the authority of Bede and the *Anglo-Saxon Chronicle*. He gives special praise to that King Caedwalla who ravaged Kent and died in Rome shortly after being baptised. Coming to the reign of Caedwalla's successor, Ine, he adds one detail not to be found in the *Chronicle*, which recorded Ine's conquest of Kent; William adds that he overcame, or at least attacked, the East Angles. He records in full Ine's deed of gift of land to Glastonbury and a similar document of his successor Aethelheard, and carries the story down to the reign of Egbert who succeeded to the kingdom of Wessex in 800.

In Chapter III William deals with the kingdom of Northumbria, and soon tells the famous story of St Gregory and the young Angles in Rome—'not Angles but Angels'. Finally he reports the despatch of Augustine's mission. Again he follows closely the accounts of the *Chronicle* and Bede, of whose life and death he gives a full narrative. 'With this man' writes William, paying tribute to one he saw as his exemplar, 'there was buried all knowledge of history down to our own times.'

He then refers to Alcuin, the English monk who lived and worked in France under Charlemagne. Alcuin's writings, quoted by William, reveal some interesting aspects of life in Bede's old monastery at Monkswearmouth. Not all the young men were as totally devoted to prayer and scholarship as the pious would wish, for Alcuin ascribes the downfall of Northumbria, which followed so soon after Bede's death, to the temporal interests of the youths in the monastery—hunting the fox and coursing the hare. We have an engaging glimpse of the young scholars out on the hills, as keen on a day's sport as their brothers and cousins in the farms of Northumbria. Because Alcuin spent much of his life in France, this passage leads William to give an account of the kings of that country and their ancestry. He ends his story of Northumbria with the coming of the Danes and the conquest of the kingdom in 827 by Egbert of Wessex.

The kings of Mercia are dealt with in Chapter IV, and the story opens with the reign of King Penda the heathen, who allied himself with the Britons and who built Mercia into a great and dominant kingdom. In addition to recounting the acts of Mercia's kings, William quotes at length a letter from St Boniface to King Aethelbald, the great-nephew of Penda. Boniface was an Englishman who became Archbishop of Metz and who met a martyr's death. His letter gives us another glimpse of everyday life in eighth-century Mercia. In words reminiscent of Gildas he vigorously rebukes King Aethelbald for unchastity:

> You wallow in lust and even adultery with nuns. What is more, I have heard that almost all the nobles in the Mercian kingdom, following your examples, desert their lawful wives and live in sinful relationships with adulteresses and nuns.

Boniface (as quoted by William) also had occasion to criticise both clergy and nuns 'for the excellence and vanity of their dress'. Ecclesiastical foundations were not quite as quiet and sober as one might have imagined from the pages of other chroniclers.

As elsewhere, William decorates his narrative with quotations from classical authors. He paints the decline of Mercia, pointing out that it ultimately fell under the dominion of Alfred, so that

> the rule of the Mercians, which had blossomed so early because of the great ambition of a heathen [King Penda], died altogether through the inactivity of an ineffective king in the year 875.

There follows a brief chapter on the kingdom of the East Angles whose foundation William places after that of Kent but earlier than Wessex. 'The first and greatest king' was Raedwald, who is mentioned by the *Anglo-Saxon Chronicle* in the year 617. Raedwald was in fact not the first East Anglian king, though undoubtedly the greatest. He slew Aethelfrith, King of Northumbria, and took the title of *Bretwalda*, or Lord of Britain. William briefly lists Raedwald's successors and tells of the death of King Edmund. The *Chronicle* merely records that the latter was killed by the Danes: 'In the same winter, King Edmund fought against them and they slew the king and occupied the whole kingdom.' William adds a detail that seems to be taken from one of the manuscripts of the *Chronicle*—Manuscript F, a copy made at Canterbury after the Conquest. For he tells us that Edmund was slain by 'Hingwar, a heathen'. He deals very briefly with the Danish occupation during the time when East Anglia formed part of the lands ceded to the Danes by Alfred, until his son Edward brought the kingdom back into his own realms.

The sixth and final chapter of Book I deals with the kings of the East Saxons, whose kingdom never achieved any position of importance. William recorded that their first king was named Sleda, tenth in descent from Woden. He makes Sleda the father of 'King Saeberht' who according to the *Chronicle* was reigning in 604, so that he places the foundation of the kingdom in the latter half of the sixth century. Saeberht received Christianity at the hands of Mellitus who had been sent by Gregory to assist

Augustine, and who became Bishop of London, principal city of the East Saxons. William follows Bede in telling us how, on Saeberht's death, his pagan sons drove Mellitus from the kingdom. But he seems to have had access to some additional source. Bede speaks of three sons, and gives none of their names. William mentions only two, and names them as Sexred and Siward who, he says, were later killed by the West Saxons. He brings the story down to the reign of Egbert and adds the interesting detail that the East Saxons lost control of London to the West Saxons.

William makes it clear that he saw the reign of Egbert of Wessex as marking a turning point in English history. Egbert led Wessex to triumphant supremacy and William saw him as the effective king of a united England.

Book II accordingly opens with an account of Egbert's life: how as a young noble, jealously regarded by King Beorhtric of Wessex, he went to King Offa of Mercia, fled to France, and on the death of Beorhtric was invited back to Wessex, and crowned king in 800. Egbert first marched against the Britons in Cornwall and, having subjugated them, turned against the Britons in the north. None of this is to be found in the *Chronicle*, William being the only authority. Thereafter, King Egbert defeated Mercia, Kent, Sussex, Essex and Surrey, and finally Northumbria; he was master of all the English kingdoms.

William describes the reign of Aethelwulf, Egbert's son, a man more fit for prayer than the sword. He personally took England's tribute—the famous 'Peter's Pence'—to Rome. He returned through France where he married Judith, daughter of Charles the Bald, King of the Franks. On his return he faced difficulties from those (including his son Aethelbald) who opposed his foreign marriage. Civil war was avoided and the kingdom divided between father and son, Aethelwulf himself restraining his supporters from resorting to arms. Again, William provides us with details not to be found in the *Anglo-Saxon Chronicle* which merely reports:

Charles, king of the Franks, gave him his daughter as queen and after that he went back to his people and they were glad. Two years after his return from the Franks, he died.

His son Aethelbald died five years later. The *Chronicle* has nothing to report of his reign. But William tells us that he was 'evil and perfidious' and married Queen Judith, his father's widow. In 867, his son Aethelred became king. William extols the greatness and the glorious manner in which he resisted the Danes, assisted by his brother Alfred. On one occasion, it was announced to King Aethelred, while he was at prayer, that the Danes were attacking. He swore, writes William, that he would move not a step until he had finished his devotions—a story which anticipates Sir Francis Drake by 700 years! William records his death—'borne down by innumerable labours'—and his burial at Wimborne.

Aethelred was, as we have seen, succeeded by his younger brother Alfred, his faithful lieutenant. William is eloquent about the new king and about the ardour of his continuous campaigns against the victorious Danes. He tells us how at length King Alfred held only 'three counties, Hampshire, Wiltshire and Somerset', and how he was forced to retreat to the Isle of Athelney. It is to William that we owe the story of Alfred visiting the camp of the Danish kings, disguised as a minstrel, and of his being taken to the Danes' banqueting hall where he saw and heard the secrets of his enemies. There is an account of the baptism of the Danish leader Guthrum and of the renewed attacks of the Danish host.

William adds one fascinating detail. Alfred was present at every battle, inspiring his soldiers by the example of his own courage. 'The exact places' wrote William 'are still pointed out by local people where he met good fortune or bad.' So that some 250 years after Alfred's death, people in the countryside still vividly remembered him and the places where he fought and laboured. William sums up the king's character and achievements in a single sentence: 'It was necessary to fight against Alfred even after he had been conquered and cast down.' In Book II, the story is taken down to the reign of King Harold Godwinson, a period outside the scope of this book.

William of Malmesbury is one of the greatest of our early historians. Like Bede, whom he admired so much, he created a coherent and well-ordered narrative from the bare chronicles from which he worked. Bede had the added greatness of being a pioneer, and of first conceiving an organised history of the English people. But William succeeded magnificently in his own purpose of bridging the gap between Bede's time and his own.

He did more. Although he based his work largely on Bede and the *Anglo-Saxon Chronicle*, he appears to have had access to other material. For example, though he felt he had too little reliable evidence to fill out the story of Arthur, he added significantly to what we can learn from Gildas and Nennius. In the same way, his account of Glastonbury throws considerable light upon its history. He gives new details for the Saxon period, and his balanced and lucid narrative is one of the great historical treasures that have come down to us.

IX

GEOFFREY OF MONMOUTH

IN 1152, some ten years after the death of William of Malmesbury, a new bishop was appointed to the See of St Asaph in Wales. His name was Geoffrey, and he is known to history as Geoffrey of Monmouth. Living and working in Wales, his main interest was in the early history of the Britons, in their vicissitudes and triumphs, in their ancient glory and their proud memories of the prowess of their legendary heroes. Just as William the Englishman wrote a book to celebrate the deeds of his Anglo-Saxon forbears, so did Geoffrey the Welshman compose a long and detailed work about his ancestors the Britons.

The two men were working at about the same time. William's *De Gestis Regum Anglorum* (*History of the Kings of England*) was completed some time before 1142; he appears to have died shortly after. Geoffrey's *Historia Britonum* (*History of the Britons*) was written some time before 1147, for it is dedicated to Robert, Earl of Gloucester, who died in that year. Both men wrote in Latin; both had the same aim—to tell the story of the folk from whom they were descended.

But their methods and styles were completely different. William—matter-of-fact, cautious, naming his two main sources, and rejecting stories that seemed to him merely fabulous; Geoffrey—imaginative, uncritical, full of fancy, and claiming a source which he does nothing to identify.

In a dedication addressed to the Earl of Gloucester Geoffrey claimed that his book was nothing more than a translation into Latin of 'a very old book written in the language of the Britons'. He does not name it, but is content to allege that it contained a history of the deeds of all the kings of the Britons

> in a consequential and ordered narrative, elegantly written, from Brutus the first king of the Britons down to Cadwallader the son of Cadwalla.

Since Geoffrey's own book takes us down to 689, his claim to have taken it from this source means, if true, that the 'very old book' covered an immense span of time—from the fall of Troy to the seventh century AD, and cannot possibly be a contemporary or reliable account for all the events of such a vast period. Yet in his 'translation' Geoffrey makes it appear that for much of the time he is able to quote the actual speeches of the heroes of the past, with other details that suggest an eye-witness account.

He was both proud and secretive about this mysterious book. At the end of his own work he refers to it again and suggests that possession of it entitles him and him alone to attempt to write of the kings of the Britons.. He tells us two things about this precious document. First, it was given to him by 'Walter, archdeacon of Oxford, a man of great learning and skilled in foreign history'. This is stated both in the dedication and in the final paragraph of Geoffrey's book. Second, it was brought by Walter from Brittany, a point made only in the conclusion.

We must reject Geoffrey's claim that his book is a simple translation of one work, partly on internal evidence—in the very first chapter describing the island there are traces of Orosius, Gildas and Bede—and partly on his second claim, also made in the dedication, that he worked, too, from verbal tradition which still survived in his day. Regretting the absence in Gildas and Bede of any reference either to the kings of Briton before Christ or to Arthur, he writes

> Their deeds were worthy of immortal fame and were celebrated by many in attractive ways, learned by heart, as if they had been written down.

This is an acceptable statement. We have seen in William's work how verbal traditions of Alfred, complete with topographical details, survived for nearly 300 years and may have persisted a good deal longer. Geoffrey's assessment of the verbal traditions which he used is interesting. They were so attractively recounted, and had so evidently been learned by heart, that it seemed to him that they must have derived from earlier written records already lost in his day. This may well be true, and the stories he heard may have been based on fragments of half-forgotten poems or barely remembered chronicles of real events, distorted by centuries of telling and retelling, and decorated by the national pride of the story tellers. At least a few genuine folk memories may be embodied in Geoffrey's work.

Similarly, it may be true that he did receive from Walter at least some written material from Brittany, where we know that the Arthurian legend survived. Geoffrey is unlikely to have identified the donor of the book so clearly were he telling a flat lie, for Walter could have denied it and totally discredited him. Unless we are prepared to believe that the archdeacon and the future bishop had engaged in a deliberate conspiracy to cheat, we must assume that there was at least some substance in Geoffrey's claim. Accordingly, his book should be regarded as a mixture of many ingredients. There are the works of Gildas and Bede, to which he refers in his preface; the works of Caradoc of Llancarfan and William of Malmesbury mentioned in his conclusion; genuine local traditions collected from 'many people'; some written material from Brittany, itself, no doubt distorted and romanticised; finally, binding all together, his own creative and tireless imagination: he invents characters with the exuberant ease of a Shakespeare or a Dickens.

It is this quality which makes his work so attractive, but which renders so difficult—if not impossible—the task of separating the drops of truth from the swelling ocean of narrative. The book opens soberly enough with the description of Britain we have already noted, and then proceeds to tell the tale of Brutus who accidentally kills his father Ascanius with an arrow and is banished, as in Nennius. We are treated to fourteen chapters of stirring adventures, with Brutus becoming commander of the Trojans, taking victorious revenge upon the Greeks, and fighting his way through Gaul. Thence he sets sail for Britain and lands at Totnes—the kind of detail that Geoffrey loved and which is so obviously quite untrue.

Britain, he notes, was then called Albion and he adds the charming detail that 'it was uninhabited except for a few giants'. Brutus renames the island Britain after himself, and he and his lieutenant Corineus proceed to rid the island of its giants. The greatest of these was Goemagot (perhaps Gogmagog, who has since become two giants, Gog and Magog). This may well be a genuine folk memory which Geoffrey has woven into his extraordinary narrative. Brutus then builds a city on the Thames which he calls New Troy. (We have already discussed the likely origins of this story.) Geoffrey adds that it was later renamed Kaer-Lud (and so London) after King Lud, brother of Cassibellann who fought Julius Caesar'. Again, we may be in the presence of a genuine tradition of a real king's name, since Caesar did indeed fight King Cassivellaunus though the details of the story are not true.

Book II opens with Brutus's death and the division of the kingdom between his sons. In course of time there reigned a king by the name of Ebraucus, a contemporary of Saul. Ebraucus founded York (Eboracum) and also distinguished himself by begetting twenty sons and thirty daughters, all of whose names the indefatigable Geoffrey was able to record!

Most notable among these was perhaps his second son Bladud who founded Bath, taught necromancy, succeeded in flying, but fell from the skies on to the Temple of Apollo in London, and so died. After this sad event (the first recorded flying accident in British history!) he was succeeded by his son Leir. Geoffrey, ever ready to find improbable evidence in almost any name, wrote that Leir founded the city of Leir-cestre, the modern Leicester! But Leir has a more enduring claim to fame, for he is no less a person than Shakespeare's King Lear. Geoffrey has the whole story, with Goneril, Regan and Cordelia, the cruelty of the two elder sisters, Cordelia's marriage in France and the king's despair. But Shakespeare has changed the tale somewhat. With Geoffrey, Leir is restored to his kingdom by Cordelia having routed his evil sons-in-law by force of arms, but poor Cordelia does not escape her fate, and is driven to suicide five years later.

Geoffrey tells us that it was after Leir's reign that Romulus and Remus built Rome, so that he is placing the story just before 753 BC. Book II closes with the reign of one Dunwallo Molmutius, whose campaigns are recounted, and who is said to have established the Molmutine Law whereby 'temples of the gods as also cities' were to give sanctuary to fugitives. Then, in Book III, we are briefly in the presence of real history, however distorted. One of the chief characters is Brennius, second son of Dunwallo Molmutius. He is evidently a shadowy representation of the real Brennius, leader of the Gauls, who captured Rome in 390 BC. According to Geoffrey he was no continental chief but a prince of Britain. Jealous of his elder brother Belinus, he went to Norway where he married the daughter of King Elsingius. He was pursued by Guichthlac, 'King of the Dacians'.

After many adventures the two brothers Belinus and Brennius are reconciled. They conquer Gaul and invade Italy. They attack the city of Rome, beseige it, set up gibbets before the gates and finally take it. The whole account, hilarious in its total disregard for either fact or probability, provides a key to Geoffrey's methods. Through all the tangle of fictional detail, through the fog of improbable names and even less probable events, the fact remains that he is recording one single true event: a man named

Brennius once captured the city of Rome.

A similar smattering of facts in a welter of fiction is to be found in Geoffrey's description of Julius Caesar's invasion of Britain, with which Book IV opens. Geoffrey had obviously read Caesar's own account, but he quite recklessly disregards the facts and builds up his own spirited narrative.

First, he has Caesar gazing out to sea from Gaul, recalling that the Romans and Britons were alike descended from Trojan stock and ruminating upon the possibility of shedding the blood of kinsfolk. He writes a letter along these lines to Cassivellaunus, the British leader mentioned by Caesar in his own work. Geoffrey does not hesitate to quote Cassivellaunus's reply in full. Because of its defiant tone, Caesar sails to Britain. He is attacked on the shore by Cassivellaunus and his numerous entourage—Belinus his counsellor, Androgeus of Trinovantum, Tenuantis of Cornwall and three minor kings named Cridious, Guerthaeth and Britael. In the fighting Caesar is attacked by Lud, brother of Cassivellaunus. Lud captures Caesar's sword (named *Crocea Mors* or Yellow Death) but is mortally wounded. He is buried in London and Caesar's sword interred with him. Caesar, defeated by the invincible Britons, retreats ignominously to Gaul.

Two years later Caesar returns. His ships strike the stakes set in the Thames by the Britons, and many thousands of his men are drowned. In the ensuing battle the Britons are again victorious, but Caesar escapes the carnage and returns to the Continent with a few men. Then a quarrel breaks out between Androgeus, the leader of London, and Cassivellaunus; Androgeus sends a letter to Caesar inviting him once more to come to Britain.

As in the story of Brennius, it will be seen that there are some particles of truth hidden away. Julius Caesar did invade Britain, was not successful on the first occasion and returned a second time. His opponent was named Cassivellaunus. The facts are sparse and overlaid with irrelevant and absurd fictional details, but they are none the less there, deeply embedded and hidden.

It is the same with the invasion of Claudius. We read of the extraordinary adventures of a Roman named Hamo who disguises himself as a Briton, joins their army and assassinates their king. The conquest of the Orkneys is also ascribed to Claudius who in fact remained in Britain for something under three weeks. Claudius sends to Rome for his daughter Gennuissa, who marries a British leader, and in whose honour Claudius builds the city of Gloucester.

The next passage of interest is a description of the papal mission said to have been invited by 'King Lucius'. Geoffrey takes the bare bones of Bede's story and clothes it with the flesh of abundant detail. He gives the names of 'two most holy teachers, Faganus and Duvanus', who were selected by the Pope to come to Britain. He even tells us how many pagan priests there were in the country—twenty-eight *flamens* and three *arch-flamens*. One suspects that he has taken the twenty-eight cities listed by Gildas, decided that each should have a *flamen* or priest, and that there should be three superiors. Each of the *flamens* was then made bishop and each of the superiors promoted to archbishop. Faganus and Duvanus return to Rome and Geoffrey claims that their acts were recorded in a book by Gildas—but no one has ever set eyes on it!

Book V opens with the death of King Lucius and deals with the assumption of power in Britain by Carausius, an historical personage who set up his independent régime in the island. Commander of the British fleet which the Romans organised in order to clear the Channel of pirates, he declared himself Emperor and ruled for a while in Britain. In real life he was murdered by his second-in-command Allectus, who was in turn defeated by Constantius Chlorus (who led a force against him from the Continent) with the help of his Praetorian Prefect Ascleipiodotus. All these persons feature in Geoffrey's story, but the parts they play are wildly distorted. Ascleipiodotus, for example, becomes King of Britain! Again, Geoffrey's story contains some elements of truth, which is almost lost in his extraordinary embellishments.

From the imaginary reign of Ascleipiodotus, Geoffrey moves back into the realm of history with an account of the persecution of the Christians by the Emperor Diocletian. He seems, in part at least, to be following Bede, for like him he names the three martyrs—Alban, Julius and Aaron. In addition, he names the priest whom Alban protected, Amphibalus. But whether he is here preserving some genuine tradition, or whether Amphibalus lived only in Geoffrey's teeming imagination, we shall never know.

There was an ancient tradition in Britain that Constantius Chlorus—the commander of the Roman expeditionary force which defeated Allectus, and father of Constantine the Great—married a British woman, Helena. In fact, Helena the mother of Constantine was almost certainly born in Drepanum, a town on the Gulf of Nicomedia in Greece. Nevertheless, the Britons liked to believe that Constantine, whose imperial career began in Britain, shared their blood. Geoffrey, as might be expected, makes the most of this. According to him there was a man named Coel, Duke of Colchester. He slew Ascleipiodotus and became king in his place (some say that he is the original 'Old King Cole'). It was his daughter Helena who married Constantius, who then inherited the kingdom on Coel's death and was in due course succeeded by his son Constantine. Again, most of Geoffrey's details are hopelessly and wildly wrong: Constantine was born long before Constantius Chlorus came to Britain; Constantius was never king of Britain but one of the Emperors of the West, and so forth. Nevertheless, there are a few historical facts in Geoffrey's narrative including the accurate detail that Constantius Chlorus died in York.

There is a surprisingly brief chapter on the reign of Constantine. We are told quite accurately that he 'organised an expedition to Rome, brought it under his control, and thereafter took the government of the whole world'. It is extraordinary that Geoffrey omits the best known events of Constantine's life: his vision of the Cross in the sky before his final battle for Rome, his building of Constantinople as the capital of the Empire of the East, and his recognition of Christianity as a legal and indeed official religion. Instead, Geoffrey treats us to the story of 'three of Helena's uncles—Leolin, Trahern and Marius' who accompanied Constantine to Rome and became senators. Trahern returned to Britain to put down a rebellion by one Octavius, 'Duke of the Wisseans', whom he first defeated, by whom he was in the end slain, and who finally ruled in Britain.

Geoffrey then moves on to the story of Maximus, the ambitious Spanish officer who in 383 tried to follow the example of Constantine, and took the legions from Britain, captured Rome and became Emperor.

In Geoffrey's story Maximus becomes Maximian and he is invited from Rome by emissaries from Britain. Five years after being given a kingdom, he 'fitted out a great fleet and called together all the armies in Britain'. He crossed into Gaul and conquered Armorica. We are told of Maximian's death in Rome at the hand of Gratian's friends. In fact the Emperor Gratian had committed suicide after being defeated by Maximus, who was killed at the battle of Aquileia by the Emperor Theodosius. Even more significant than these typical inaccuracies is the meagre brevity of Geoffrey's story, for Maximus held a proud place in the traditions and folklore of the Britons, and we might have expected a fuller tale.

Book VI opens with the attacks of the 'Scots, Picts, Norwegians, Dacians and others' against the defenceless island of Britain. Geoffrey gives an account of the appeal to the Consul Aetius by the desperate Britons, taken almost word for word from Gildas—even to the wrong spelling of the Consul's name. He adds some matter of his own: the Britons send Guethelin, Archbishop of London, to Brittany to seek aid from their kinsman there. Can this perhaps be based on truth? By Geoffrey's day, an Archbishop of London would have been a difficult person to invent—the traditions of Canterbury were too well known for a tale to be believed. Is Guethelin the shadow of some real British prelate who made the perilous journey to Brittany, across seas on which the ships of the Saxon pirates could at any moment appear? Or is he another child of Geoffrey's imagination?

Following the golden examples of Constantine and Maximus the Britons created yet another emperor. He was a private soldier called Constantine, and Geoffrey gives us a very brief account of his reign. He ascribes three sons to Constantine—Constans, Aurelius Ambrosius and Uther Pendragon. On Constantine's death, there was a dispute between Ambrosius and Uther Pendragon, and the issue was settled by 'Vortigern, consul of the Gewissans'. He gave the crown to Constans, the third son, who was a monk and himself performed the coronation ceremony. Again there is a mixture of fact and fable. The usurper Constantine certainly had a son named Constans who was a monk, but he died in Gaul with his father, and therefore he could not have succeeded him.

Having thus introduced Vortigern, Geoffrey makes a villain of him from the start. By cunning and treachery Vortigern conspired against Constans, invited the Picts into Britain, had Constans murdered, and became king in his place. There follows an account of the coming of the Saxons under Hengist and Horsa. Vortigern hears of the arrival of the three ships and sends for the tall strangers. Hengist explains that their own lands were over-populated and that they had been selected by lot to go abroad to seek their fortune. Vortigern invites them to help him in his wars with the Picts. They do so, and are successful. So far the story is fairly close to that of Gildas. But Geoffrey adds his usual embellishments. Hengist modestly asks for such land as can be encompassed by a single thong and, his request being granted, cuts a whole bull's hide into a single thong and so takes enough land whereon to build a castle. We have the story of the marriage of Hengist to Vortigern's daughter, as given by Nennius, and the ceding of the kingdom of Kent as a wedding gift to him.

After a digression on St Germanus, Geoffrey resumes the story of Vortigern and gives his account of the feast at which Hengist's men murdered the unsuspecting Britons. In his account they fight back resolutely and to good effect. 'Eldol, Consul of Gloucester' took up a stake and 'every blow he gave carried death . . . and he did not move from the place until with his weapon he had slain seventy men'. The exaggeration of the number slain by this one champion is reminiscent of the style of the poetry of the Britons. Is Geoffrey here echoing some ancient song, containing a traditional account of the affray?

There follows an account of a search made by Vortigern for a 'boy without a father' with whose blood the foundations of his fortress are to be sprinkled. In a complicated prophecy, the lad foretells that the Britons will in the end drive out the Saxons from their island, beating them back over the sea. The passage is taken from Nennius, enlarged upon and confused by Geoffrey's power of invention.

Book VII deals with the prophecies of Merlin. These are couched in fanciful and obscure language, and Geoffrey claims to have translated them from the British tongue into Latin. To begin with the contents have some contact with reality. 'A preacher of Ireland shall be struck dumb because of a child growing in the womb' is a sentence that suggests that the author had read of Gildas finding himself unable to preach before St David's mother, and so helps us to glimpse one of the sources of Geoffrey's material. Similarly, there are references to the struggle between the Red Dragon and the White, representing the Britons and the Saxons, and some at least of these obviously derive from Nennius. But the language grows wilder and interpretation more and more impossible. Fox, boar and wolf, together with serpent, lion and owl stalk through the pages in a nightmare medley. The whole passage is reminiscent of Nostradamus, the medieval French prophet, whose works have from generation to generation found new readers, as successive interpreters have confidently found in them references to Napoleon, Hitler and each new peril of the world. But these marvels are matters not for historians but for astrologers and those skilled in understanding the riddles of oracles.

Book VIII continues the story of Vortigern, and his death at the hands of Aurelius who besieges him in a tower. The tower is finally set on fire and Vortigern perishes in the flames. Aurelius then resumes the war against Hengist who is captured and beheaded. Part of this narrative, as with other of Geoffrey's stories, may contain elements of truth. The death of Hengist is not recorded in the *Anglo-Saxon Chronicle*, but obliquely hinted at in the entry for 488:

> In this year Aesc [Hengist's son] succeeded to the kingdom and was king of the people of Kent for twenty-four years.

If Hengist had indeed died ignominiously as a prisoner, then this silence on his death is understandable.

Geoffrey tells the story of Hengist's son Aesc, whom he calls Octa. This is the same version of the name as is used by Nennius, and again we have a hint of Geoffrey's source. But he adds details not to be found in the works of Nennius, and we are left to speculate whether he is recording traditions drawn from elsewhere or merely inventing. Ambrosius is succeeded by his brother Uther who is attacked by the Saxons and who makes Octa his captive.

We then move to magical matters. Uther falls in love with Igerna, wife of the Duke of Cornwall. Merlin miraculously transforms Uther into the likeness of the Duke and he enters the castle of Tintagel and lies with Igerna. 'She refused him nothing which he desired. The same night therefore she conceived the most renowned Arthur.' We have come a long way from the simple narrative of Nennius and Arthur the soldier, victor of Mount Badon. The hero of the Britons has taken his first steps out of the dimensions of history into the fairyland of legend and fable, where William of Malmesbury tells us that he had searched for the true Arthur in vain.

Having brought Arthur on to the stage in this romantic manner, in Book IX Geoffrey gives his version of the heroic resistance maintained by the Britons under his leadership. According to Geoffrey, Arthur succeeded to the kingdom on the death of Uther Pendragon and was crowned when he was only fifteen years old. He marched northward to York where he fought a battle against a mixed army of Saxons, Scots and Picts by the River Duglas. This is clearly an echo of Nennius, whose list of Arthur's battles includes one by a River Dubglas. Geoffrey then gives a circumstantial account of Arthur's relief of the city of 'Kaerlindcoit'. (The city's name seems to be an echo of a battle in a wood—*coit*. Is it some forgotten battle at Lincoln—*Cair Lind Coit*? This of course is pure speculation.) He drove off the besieging army of Saxons and surrounded them in 'the wood of Celidon', another echo of Nennius. Driven out by hunger, they surrendered to Arthur who imposed terms upon them whereby they returned to Germany, leaving hostages and all their treasure with him.

In a further battle, after 'girding on his Caliburn, which was an excellent sword made in the Isle of Avallon', he attacked a Saxon army who retreated as dusk fell. Next day 'he drew out his Caliburn'. He attacked with such fury that 'with his Caliburn alone' he killed 470 men.

Was Caliburn a real weapon and is Geoffrey, in these chapters, merely enlarging and embellishing the account given by Nennius? Or had he perhaps access to some other source, either written or oral, in which details were given? On the whole the name of the sword, the reference to the Isle of Avallon and the detail of a battle lasting two days, seems to derive from some unknown original. They have a circumstantial air and seem too disjointed to be the products of smooth and skilful imagination.

There follow a series of startling incidents which at first glance appear utterly to discredit Geoffrey as a serious historian; he tells how Arthur fitted out a fleet, subdued Norway, Dacia, Aquitaine and Gaul, beseiged Paris and held his court there, slew his adversary Flollo the Tribune with his sword Caliburn, and triumphed far and wide on the Continent. Afterwards he returned to Britain, celebrating the feast of Pentecost at the City of the Legions. He was there attended by numerous kings, whose names are listed.

At this time Arthur received a stern letter from 'Lucius Tiberius, Procurator of the Roman State', who called Arthur an insolent tyrant, demanded tribute, and ordered him to appear at Rome to undergo such sentence as the Roman authorities might pronounce. Arthur then held a council with all the kings of Britain who unanimously agreed that Britain must defy the messengers from Rome and stoutly prepare for war.

Book X gives an account of the struggle that took place, with Arthur everywhere triumphant. Before sailing for the Continent, Arthur placed his nephew Modred in charge of the government of Britain. In the course of their march across Europe, Arthur's armies were attacked by the Romans, who are put to flight, Lucius Tiberius, hearing of this terrible disaster, himself marched out of Rome at the head of an army. In the battle which follows he is killed. It is self-evident that if anything of this kind had happened during the sixth century, the story would have found a place in the accounts of other chroniclers. Such dramatic events as the destruction of a Roman army by forces from Britain could not possibly have gone unrecorded. The whole story seems to be pure invention and Geoffrey, as a result of this passage alone, seems to have forfeited any claims he might have had to be a serious historian.

Yet there is another possibility. Although events of this kind did not take place during the days of Arthur, we must remember that similar events had occurred about a century and a half earlier. Maximus, the ambitious commander of the Roman garrison in Britain, had indeed marched his legions to the ports of Britain, embarked them in the transports and landed them on the Continent. There he had defeated a Roman army and had been crowned Emperor in Rome itself. The story told by Geoffrey about Arthur could in fact be his recording of a confused folk-memory of the high adventure of Maximus. Geoffrey could have found this in Brittany, whence he claimed to have drawn his material. And the story (basically true) might have become attached to the name of a different hero, to Arthur and not to Maximus, as can happen with matters preserved by verbal tradition, handed on from generation to generation and distorted in the telling. Should this be so, then Geoffrey may be accurately recording (and no doubt embellishing) the inaccurate folk-memories that he had heard. If so, he stands absolved of the charge of irresponsible fabrication. Certainly, much of the detail of his story about Arthur would perfectly fit all that we know about Maximus.

In Book XI, Geoffrey repeats his claim to be working from a British book given to him by Walter, archdeacon of Oxford, and then tells us of Arthur's return to Britain. Modred had proved to be a traitor, sending Chelderic, a Saxon leader, into Germany to raise fresh forces to fight against Arthur. The armies of Modred and Arthur met. Modred died in the battle which followed and Arthur was mortally wounded. We know of this engagement, the Battle of Camlan, from the *Welsh Annals*. But Geoffrey seems to be using a different source, for he adds one detail not to be found in that work—that after the battle Arthur was carried to the Isle of Avallon to be cured of his wounds and gave the crown of Britain to a kinsman named Constantine, son of the Duke of Cornwall. Moreover, he ascribes the battle to the year 542, whereas the *Welsh Annals* gives the year as 537.

There follows a series of short chapters telling us of the reign of Arthur's successor, Constantine. Stonehenge, according to Geoffrey, was erected as his tomb! Three or four kings later we find Britain most improbably invaded by a joint force of Saxons and Africans, the latter led by their king Gormund who had previously invaded Ireland. Book XI closes with a brief account of Augustine's mission to Britain.

Book XII is on firmer ground. We have a somewhat confused

account of the reign of King Edwin, the first Christian king of Northumbria and of Cadwalla, King of the Britons. Again fact and fancy are mixed. Cadwalla is cured of his sickness by being fed a slice of roast meat, cut by his nephew Brian from his own thigh. Edwin has a magician, Pellitus, whom Brian slays. The reign of Penda and his death in battle is also recorded. The juxtaposition of historical truth with evident fancy in Geoffrey's account of this later period entitles us to assume that his story of the days of Vortigern and Arthur are of a like nature, and we must not reject out of hand everything that he tells us.

Geoffrey ends his work with an admonishment to other historians

> to be silent concerning the kings of the Britons, since they have not that book, written in the British tongue, which Walter, archdeacon of Oxford brought out of Brittany, and which—being a true history drawn up in honour of those princes—I have thus carefully translated.

Had Geoffrey been born in modern times, he might have been a successful novelist. If Bede can be called the father of English history, perhaps Geoffrey is entitled to be known as the father of historical fiction. Even from the works of historical novelists, some understanding of history can be gleaned. And as we have seen, Geoffrey's book may contain a few fragments of truth which are not recorded elsewhere.

Much of what he wrote has become part of British folklore if not of history and was taught in schools as recently as a generation ago. And the man who provided Shakespeare with the plot of *King Lear* has surely earned himself a place among the chroniclers.

EPILOGUE

THE works we have examined are virtually the only written evidence composed in Britain itself for events there during the Dark Ages. For the Roman period there were writers on the Continent who recorded something of what was happening in the remote island—we have already glanced at the works of Caesar and Tacitus. But they, with such authors as Strabo and Cassius Dio, were writing before the shadows of the Dark Ages fell across Britain, and at a time when the full light of history still shone. For the first decades of the Dark Ages proper, that is to say from about AD 400 onwards, there were also a few writers on the Continent who continued to mention something of what was happening in the lost province.

Zosimus, a Greek writer who was working some time between AD 450 and 501, tells us briefly that in his day 'the barbarians from across the Rhine, ravaging as they pleased, compelled the inhabitants of Britain . . . to leave the Roman Empire'. He records, too, the last message sent by Rome over the signature of the Emperor Honorius to the States of Britain exhorting them to look to their own defences. Another continental chronicle, attributed (wrongly) to Prosper Tiro, also records the devastation of Britain by the Saxons. But these and similar references are scant and give only a blurred picture of events.

Gildas is the only witness to provide abundant (though imperfect) evidence for this period. The whole of his work was written during the time when the Saxons and Britons were bitterly fighting for possession of the island. Whatever view is taken of the accuracy of his work as history, there can be no doubt that he speaks with the authentic voice of the sixth-century Britons struggling against the savage might of the Anglo-Saxons. If, during the centuries that followed his death, the value of his work was overestimated, it is probably also true that his evidence in recent years has been too heavily discounted. His self-evident and abundant errors of fact prevent us from taking all his narrative as true in detail, but we can certainly accept him as an eyewitness of much that he described, and as a repository of the traditions and beliefs of the Britons. He accurately records the mood, the despair and the sense of doom which oppressed sixth-century Britain. His story in its outline rings true, and we are fortunate to possess such a record, however faulty in detail, of the struggle between the two contending races, and of the spirit of the times.

The works of Nennius also have much that is authentic history. Although the document as it is today probably dates from 150 years or so after the time of Gildas, much of it is drawn from very early and probably contemporary sources. The work supplements, and in part corroborates, the writings of Gildas, and gives us some details that are not to be found in Gildas's story. It is to Nennius, for example, that we owe the first unambiguous reference to Arthur, and to his great victory at Badon. This battle, incidentally, has for too long been left in the shadows. Perhaps it ought to take its place in our history books ranking with Mons and Dunkirk. Much of Nennius's work for example the prophecies of the boy Merlin—are myths rather than history. Nevertheless, they contain elements of truth not to be found elsewhere.

The *Welsh Annals* and the *Chronicles of the Princes of Wales* represent the later voice of the defeated and isolated Britons. Both—and particularly the former—contain invaluable items of information. It is from the *Welsh Annals*, for example, that we know when Gildas was writing, the date of his death, and the date of Arthur's last and tragic battle at Camlan.

When Christianity came to the English towards the end of the sixth century, literacy and the desire to record in writing the traditions of the nation's beginning followed surprisingly swiftly. The *Anglo-Saxon Chronicle* is an enduring monument to the rapidity with which the English became articulate. We have to accept that the first section, dealing with events which took place at least 200 years before any record was begun, represents an account of traditions rather than of firm historical facts. Even so, this early section is invaluable. The accuracy of verbal tradition, particularly among primitive peoples, must never be underestimated. We may take the early entries of the *Anglo-Saxon Chronicle* as accurately representing what the later Anglo-Saxons believed (and perhaps knew) of the way in which they had come to the island, and the manner in which they set up their many kingdoms. We may with some certainty accept that the basic story is true, for it does not conflict with the contemporary records of Gildas and Nennius. For the later period the *Anglo-Saxon Chronicle* is a superb document. Minor inaccuracies there inevitably are, but taken as a whole it represents an almost perfect record of all the major events in the kingdom, written by men to whom those events were part of the pattern of their daily lives, and it was maintained for many centuries.

The conversion to Christianity of King Edwin of Northumbria (who reigned from 617 to 633) marked a turning-point in English scholarship. The northern English took to the arts of writing and history as to the manner born. It is no disrespect to folk in the south to say that it was in Northumbria that learning reached its fine flowering. Even King Alfred, a man of Wessex, when writing of the decay of learning brought about by the long wars with the Danes, made the comment that knowledge had faded even north of the Humber, and this seemed to shock him. Within a century of Edwin's conversion, monasteries had been established, and to some of them schools were attached. Bede's

Ecclesiastical History of the English People was written in this atmosphere, and his whole work is bathed in the clear light of abundant scholarship. It is a superb document which later writers of the *Anglo-Saxon Chronicle* were happy to use as a source. The *Chronicle* and Bede's *History* are the two finest works available to us for the later part of the Dark Ages.

King Alfred—soldier, administrator and scholar—brought the *Anglo-Saxon Chronicle* to a new peak of achievement, and gave it such impetus that it was maintained for over 250 years after his death. The account of his life by Asser cannot rank with the *Chronicle* itself for reliability, nor with Bede for erudition. But it is an engaging work, conversational and intimate in tone, drawing a clear picture of King Alfred—restless, energetic and impatient of others' ignorance; ailing and in frequent pain, but untiring in his work of governing a kingdom devastated by war, and of restoring within it the arts of peace and the love of learning. Some of the anecdotes are no doubt apocryphal, inserted by later hands. It is a book that must be used with caution, but it must be read.

After the Normans conquered England the nation began to look back with pride at its former glories and achievements. This was the background to the work of William of Malmesbury, unashamedly written to celebrate the greatness of his people. To that extent it is an early essay in the romantic style of history, but it is carefully done, making use of all the sources we know, and perhaps of others now lost. In his accurate use of older material he can be compared with Bede whom he admired so much. Moreover, his knowledge of the classical authors whom he so frequently quoted shows the extent to which a knowledge of the ancient world still persisted in the cloisters of England's monasteries. William of Malmesbury's familiarity with the writers of Greece and Rome seems to anticipate by 400 years something of the spirit of the Renaissance, and provides an interesting commentary on the neat but misleading labels attached to different ages by historians.

The last writer to be considered, Geoffrey of Monmouth, is to be placed somewhere on the frontier that divides history and fiction, yet he is not to be despised. It is evident that part at least of his narrative is based on genuine facts. Real persons appear, acting roles ludicrously different from those they played in real life. Yet among all the fantasies a few grains of truth remain to be winnowed. If our own civilisation were engulfed by disaster, and all records destroyed save the works of some historical novelist, later ages would know at least something of the world we lived in. The names of kings and of cities, the places where great battles were fought—from these things, much might be deduced. Yet Geoffrey has earned his place among the historians more by the power and dash of his imagination than by his accuracy or scholarship.

The times we have looked at were, for the first two or three centuries, dark indeed. The fog of war, the clouds of despair, the boastful glare of triumphant armies and the mourning candles of the defeated—in the shadows and light of all these, the truth is seen fitfully and confusedly. But with such guides as Gildas and Bede, the writers of the *Welsh Annals* and the *Anglo-Saxon Chronicle*, Bishop Asser and William of Malmesbury, much is made clear. And if sometimes we are led away into the twilit landscape of legend and imagination, even then our journey is not without profit.

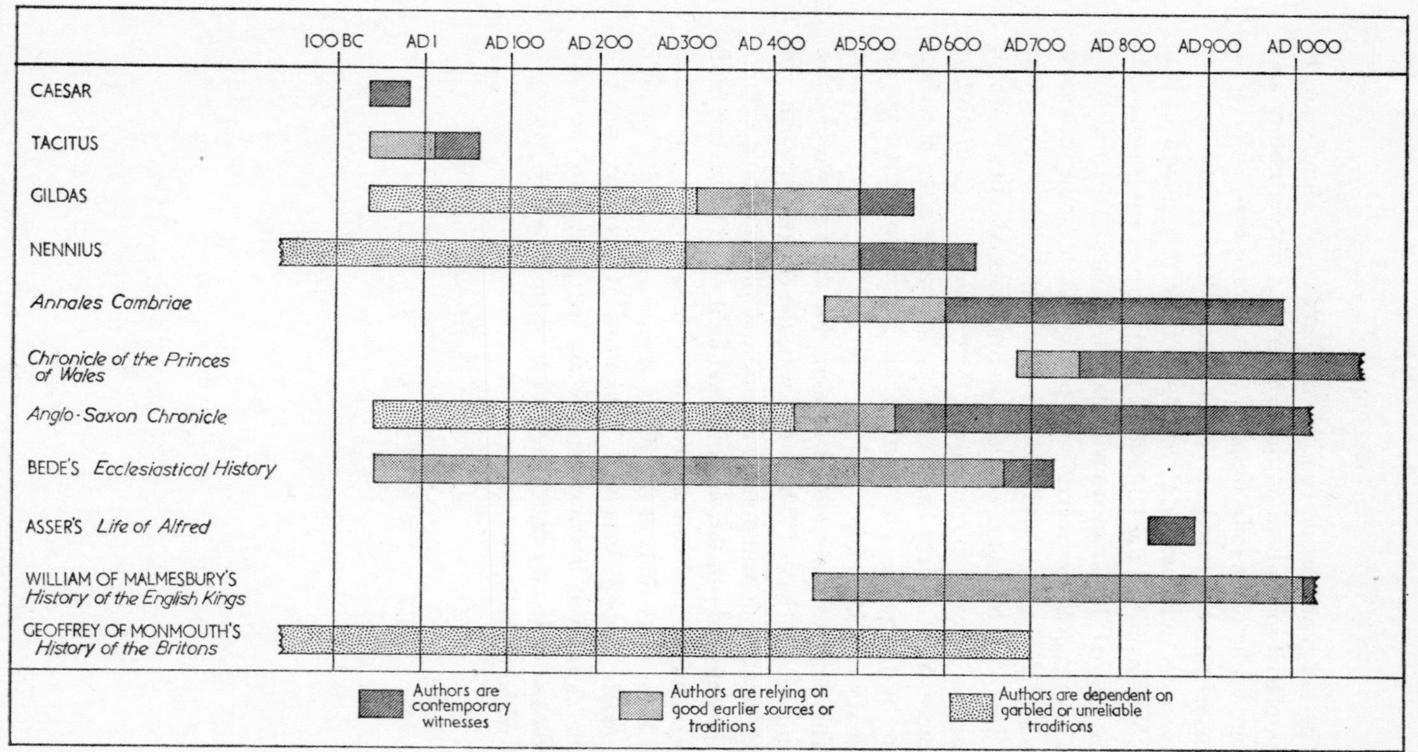

THE PERIODS COVERED BY THE CHRONICLES
The divisions between reliability and unreliability are of course approximate and indeed a little arbitrary

NOTE ON TEXTS AND TRANSLATIONS

THE full texts, together with English translations, of all the chroniclers considered in this book are available today.

Interest in them began to develop very early. The text of Gildas's *De Excidio Britanniae* was first printed in 1525 by Polydore Vergil. It was reprinted in 1568 by John Josseline, secretary to Archbishop Parker. The works of Nennius were included in a book entitled *Quindecim Scriptores* by Gale in 1691 and Edmund Gibson (who later became Bishop of London) published a text of the *Anglo-Saxon Chronicle* in 1692.

Bede's *Historia Ecclesiastica Gentis Anglorum* was first printed in the late fifteenth century by Conrad Fyner at Eslingen and two further editions came out in Strasbourg a few years thereafter.

The text of Asser's *Life of King Alfred* was published by Archbishop Parker in 1574. The text of Aethelweard was brought out by Sir Henry Savile in 1596, as part of a book entitled *Scriptores post Bedam.*

In more recent times, the House of Commons addressed a petition to George IV 'praying that His Majesty would be pleased to give such directions as he might think fit for the publication of a complete Edition of the ancient Histories of this Realm.' It was envisaged that there would be several volumes, dealing with the history of Britain from the earliest period to the end of the reign of King Henry VII. Volume I (all that was ever published) was to end with the Norman Conquest. The work on this volume was entrusted to Henry Petrie (Keeper of the Records in the Tower of London), who died before the task was completed. He was assisted by John Sharpe, a Wiltshire clergyman, and on Petrie's death, Thomas Duffus Hardy completed the work. Volume I was eventually published in 1848, in folio, dedicated to Queen Victoria and entitled *Monumenta Historica Britannica.* It contains, amongst other texts, the works of Gildas, the *Annales Cambraie*, the *Brut y Tywysogion*, the *Anglo-Saxon Chronicle*, Bede's *Historia Ecclesiastica Gentis Anglorum* and Asser's *De Gestis Alfredi.* The texts are carefully edited and the variant readings from the different manuscripts are noted. It is a fine piece of work, and provides a complete source-book for the earliest period of Britain's history. Copies are still available in many libraries.

Modern editions are also available for most of the authors. The texts of Gildas and Nennius were published in London in 1823 by Stevenson. Both appear in translation in *Six Early English Chroniclers* published in the Bohn Library in 1861.

The text of the *Annales Cambriae* (without a translation) was published by Her Majesty's Stationery Office in 1860, edited by John Williams ab Ithel, Rector of Llanymowddwy; an excellent facsimile reprint was published in Germany in 1965 by Kraus Reprint Limited.

A translation of the *Brut y Tywysogion* by T. Jones has been published by the University of Wales, who have also published the Welsh text, based on the *Red Book of Hergest*, a fourteenth-century manuscript at Jesus College, Oxford.

There is an excellent modern English version of the *Anglo-Saxon Chronicle* in Dent's Everyman's Library, translated and edited by G. N. Garmonsway who has printed translations of the different manuscripts, so that one can see at a glance the variations between them. The original Anglo-Saxon text is published by the Oxford University Press, in two volumes, edited by

Plummer and Earle.

The English translation of Bede's *Historia Ecclesiastica Gentis Anglorum*, by Leo Sherley-Price, is published in the Penguin Classics. For those who wish to see the original Latin text as well, *Baedae Opera Historica* published by Heinemann in the Loeb Classics gives the original text side by side with an English translation by J. E. King.

Asser's *Life of Alfred*, edited by W. H. Stevenson, was published in 1959 by the Oxford University Press.

There is a good translation of William of Malmesbury's *De Gestis Regum Anglorum* in the Bohn Library by J. A. Giles, published in 1847.

A translation of Geoffrey of Monmouth's *Historia Regum Britanniae* is available in the Everyman Library (translated by Evans and Dunn) and also in the Penguin Classics, translated by Lewis Thorpe.

KEY TO PLATES

Page 49 (*left*) Part of a page from the works of Gildas. This is a page from the manuscript in the Cambridge University Library (F, f, 1, 27). Known as Manuscript A: It dates from about the end of the twelfth century. It is written on vellum, medium folio in double columns. The plate shows the opening words of Gildas's work and a translation reads:

> The island of Britain, situated on almost the utmost border of the earth, towards the south and west, and poised in the divine balance, as it is said, which supports the whole world, stretches out from the south-west towards the north pole, and is eight hundred miles long and two hundred broad, except where the headlands of sundry promontories stretch farther into the sea. It is surrounded by the ocean, which forms winding bays, and is strongly defended by this ample, and, if I may so call it, impassable barrier, save on the south side, where the narrow sea affords a passage to Belgic Gaul. It is enriched by the mouths of two noble rivers, the Thames and the Severn, as it were two arms, by which foreign luxuries were of old imported, and by other streams of less importance.

Page 49 (*right*) Part of Folio 94 of a manuscript of Bede's *Historia Ecclesiastica Gentis Anglorum* in the British Museum (Cotton Tiberius C ii). This manuscript was made in the late eighth century, probably in South England. The following is a translation of the passage shown:

> In the above-mentioned year, when there was an eclipse, swiftly followed by a plague, during which Colman was defeated by the unanimous arguments of the Catholics and returned to his own folk, Deusdedit the sixth Bishop of the church in Canterbury died on the day before the Ides of July [14 July]. But Erconberct King of Kent, dying in the same month and on the same day, left his royal seat to his son Ecgberct.

Page 50 Folio 192 of the most important manuscript of the *Annales Cambriae*. The manuscript, (Harleian 3859), which is in the British Museum, is written in Latin on vellum in octavo, and is inserted without title or introduction into the works of Nennius. It dates from the end of the tenth century to the beginning of the eleventh century.

The manuscript is written in three columns. The page shown covers the years AD 784 to 844 and the following is a translation:

Column 1
(784) CCCXL
A devastation of the Britons by Offa in the summer.
(795) CCCLI
The first coming of the pagans into the righthand of Britain (South Wales).
(796) CCCLII
Offa, King of the Mercians, Margetiud, King of Demetia, died; and there was the battle of Rudglann.
(798) CCCLIV
Caratauc King of Guenedote was slaughtered among the Saxons.
(807) CCCLXIII
Arthgen, King of Cereticiaun

Column 2
died.
(808) CCCLXIV
Regin, King of Dimetia and Catell King of Powys, died
(809) CCCCLXV

Elbodg, Archbishop of the Kingdom Guenedote, went to the Lord.

(810) CCCLXVI

The burning of Miniu.

(811) CCCLXVII

Eugem, son of Margetieud, died.

(812) CCCLXVIII

The Region of the Decanti was burned by a thunderbolt.

(813) CCCLXIX

A battle between . . . Higuel was the victor.

(814) CCCLXX

There were great thunderstorms and there were many fires. Trifun, son of Regin, died. And Griphiud, son of Cincen, having come under the cunning control of his brother, Elized, was slain after an interval of two months. Higuel was triumphant in the Isle of Mona and Cinan drove him thence with sorrow, with his great army.

(816) CCCLXXII

Higuel

Column 3

was again driven out of Mona. King Cinan died.

(817) CCCLXXIII

The battle of Lannmaes.

(822) CCCLXXVIII

The stronghold of the Decanti was destroyed by the Saxons and they brought the kingdom of Powys under their power.

(825) CCCLXXXI

Higuel died.

(831) CCCLXXXVI

Laudent died and Satur, Bishop of Miniu, died.

(840) CCCXCVI

Nobis reigned as Bishop in Miniu.

(842) CCCXCVIII

Iudguoll died.

(844) CCCC

Mermin died. The battle of Cetill.

Page 67 A page from the copy of the *Annales Cambriae* made on the flyleaves of an abridged copy of *Domesday Book* in the Public Record Office. The manuscript is written in Latin in three columns, and dates from the thirteenth century. Each line is headed with the word 'Annus' (Year). The entries on this page go from AD 458 down to 582. The following is a translation:

Column 1
(458) XIV
St David was born in the thirteenth year after the departure of Patrick from Menevia.
(468) XXIV
Death of Benignus the Bishop.
(501) LVII
Bishop Ebur died in Christ in the three hundred and fiftieth year of his age.

Column 2
(516) LXXII
The Battle of Badon in which King Arthur bore the cross of our Lord Jesus Christ for three days and three nights upon his shoulders. In this battle there fell Colgrinus and Radulph, leaders of the English.
(521) LXXVII
St Columchilla was born. St Brigid died in Christ.
(537) XCIII
The Battle of Camlann in which the famous Arthur, King of the Britons and Modred his kinsman died of the wounds they gave one another.

Column 3
(544) C
Death of Karaun.
(547) CIII
There was a great mortality in Britain in which died Mailguin, King of Guineth from which it is said '*Hir hun Wailgun en llis Ros*' [Long is the sleep of Maelgwn in the court of Ros]. There was an outbreak of the Yellow Plague.
(558) CXIV
Gabran, son of Dungart, died.
(562) CXVIII
Columchilla came from Ireland into Britain.

(565) CXXI
Journey of Gildas into Ireland.
(569) CXXV
The Synod of Victory was convened among the Britons.
(570) CXXVI
Gildas the wisest of the Britons died.
(573) CXXIX
The Battle of Erderit between the sons of Elifer and Guendolen the son of Keidiau, in which battle Guendolen fell. Merlin became insane.
(574) CXXX
Brendan Beror died.
(580) CXXXVI
Guurci and Peretur the sons of Elifer died.

Page 68 This is a page from one of the oldest known manuscripts of the works of Nennius. Known as Manuscript A (Harleian 3859), it is in the British Museum, and is written on vellum, late tenth or early eleventh century. In it is inserted, without title or introduction, a manuscript of the *Annales Cambriae*.

The illustration shows the final paragraphs of chapter 17, the whole of chapter 18, and the beginning of chapter 19. The translation reads:

[The first man that dwelt in Europe was] Alanus, with his three sons, Hisicion, Armenon, and Neugio. Hisicion had four sons, Francus, Romanus, Alamanus, and Brutus. Armenon had five sons, Gothus, Valagothus, Cibidus, Burgundus, and Longobardus. Neugio had three sons, Vandalus, Saxo, and Boganus. From Hisicion arose four nations—the Franks, the Latins, the Germans, and Britons: from Armenon, the Gothi, Valagothi, Cibidi, Burgundi, and Longobardi: from Neugio, the Bogari, Vandali, Saxones and Tarinegi. The whole of Europe was subdivided into these tribes.

Alanus is said to have been the son of Fethuir; Fethuir, the son of Ogomuin, who was the son of Thoi; Thoi was the son of Boibus, Boibus of Semion, Semion of Mair, Mair of Ecthactus, Ecthactus of Aurthack, Aurthack of Ethec, Ethec of Ooth, Ooth of Aber, Aber of Ra, Ra of Esraa, Esraa of Hisrau, Hisrau of

Bath, Bath of Jobath, Jobath of Joham, Joham of Japheth, Japheth of Noah, Noah of Lamech, Lamech of Mathusalem, Mathusalem of Enoch, Enoch of Jared, Jared of Malalehel, Malalehel of Cainan, Cainan of Enos, Enos of Seth, Seth of Adam, and Adam was formed by the living God. We have obtained this information respecting the original inhabitants of Britain from ancient tradition.

18. The Britons were thus called from Brutus: Brutus was the son of Hisicion, Hisicion was the son of Alanus, Alanus was the son of Rhea Silvia, Rhea Silvia was the daughter of Numa Pompilius, Numa was the son of Ascanius, Ascanius of Eneas, Eneas of Anchises, Anchises of Troius, Troius of Dardanus, Dardanus of Flisa, Flisa of Juuin, Juuin of Japheth; but Japheth had seven sons; from the first named Gomer, descended the Galli; from the second, Magog, the Scythi and Gothi; from the third, Madian, the Medi; from the fourth, Juuan, the Greeks; from the fifth, Tubal, arose the Hebrei, Hispani, and Itali; from the sixth, Mosoch, sprung the Cappadoces; and from the seventh, named Tiras, descended the Thraces: these are the sons of Japheth, the son of Noah, the son of Lamech.

19. The Romans having obtained the dominion of the world, sent legates or deputies to the Britons to demand of them hostages and tribute, which they received from all other countries and islands; but they, fierce, disdainful, and haughty, treated the legation with contempt.

(The translation is taken from *Six Old English Chronicles* edited by J. A. Giles, D.C.L., published by Bell and Daldy, 1866.)

Page 117 From a late twelfth- or early thirteenth-century manuscript of *Historia Britonum* by Nennius. Written in Latin upon vellum in small quarto (Cottonian, Vespasian, D XXI), it is in the British Museum. It is without title and opens with the text shown on the plate. The following is a translation:

The island of Britain is so named from a certain Brutus, a Roman Consul. It rises up from Africa in the south and is turned towards the west. It is 800 miles in length and 200 miles in breadth. In it are twenty-eight cities and innumerable promontories with numerous castles built of stone and brick. And four nations inhabit it, the Scots, the Picts, the Saxons and the Britons. It has three large islands of which one faces Armorica and is called the Isle of Wight. The second is situated in the midst of the sea between Ireland and Britain and it is called by the name of Eubonia, that is, Man. The third is situated at the extreme end of Britain, beyond the Picts, and is Ork [the Orkneys]. Thus it was said in an ancient proverb, referring to its rulers or kings 'he reigned over Britain with its three islands'.

There are in it many rivers, which flow from all parts, that is, to the east, to the west, to the south, to the north. But two of these are more famous than the other rivers, and these are the Thames and Severn which, as if they are the two arms of Britain, formerly carried the ships and brought the wealth that was earned in commerce. The Britons once were very numerous and governed from sea to sea.

If anyone wishes to know how this island was inhabited during the period after the flood, I have found two separate explanations. It is written as follows in the records of the Romans themselves: Aeneas, after the Trojan War, with Ascinius his son, came to Italy, and on the death of Turnus married Lavinia, the daughter of Latinus, the son of Faunus, the son of Picus, the son of Saturn. And he inherited the kingdoms both of the Romans and of the Latins. Moreover Aeneas founded the city of Alba and after he had taken Lavinia to wife, she gave birth to a son named Silvius. Silvius also took a wife and she became pregnant and it was announced to Aeneas that she was pregnant. And he sent . . .

Page 118 This is the first sheet of the *Peterborough Chronicle* (known as Manuscript E) of the *Anglo-Saxon Chronicle*. It was once the property of Archbishop Laud, whose name appears in ink on the page shown, and it is now in the Bodleian Library, Oxford. It is written in Anglo-Saxon. The page is the introduction to the main *Chronicle* and opens with a description of the island of Britain, largely drawn from Nennius. The translation is as follows:

Britain's island is eight hundred miles long and two hundred broad. And here there are in this island five languages, English and British and Welsh and Pictish and Irish and book-Latin. The first people to dwell in this land were the British who came out of Armenia* and they first took the southward part of Britain. Then it happened that the Picts came out of the south from Scythia with longships—not many—and then they came up to northern Ireland. And there they asked the Scots if they might stay there but they did not wish them to live there. For the Scots said to them: 'We can however teach you good advice. We know of another island here to the eastward where you may settle if you will. And if any one stands against you we will help you to conquer.' Then went the Picts and took this land to the northward. The southern part was held by the British as we have already said. And then the Picts asked for wives from the Scots and these were given to them if they chose their royal kin on their wives' side and they held to this custom for a long time. Then it happened that after some years a part of the Scots went from Ireland into Britain and conquered part of that land. And the leader of their host was called Reoda and from this they are called Dael Reodi. Sixty years before Christ was born Gaius Julius, Caesar of the Romans, then sought Britain with a hundred and eighty ships. Then he was at first with fierce fighting and lost a great part of his forces. And then he . . . .

Page 135 Folio 70, from Manuscript Kk 5 16 in the Cambridge University Library, of Bede's *Historia Ecclesiastica Gentis Anglorum*, written in Latin. Known as the 'Moore' Manuscript, this is a very ancient version, dating to within a few years of Bede's death. P. Hunter Blair, in his introduction to the facsimile edition of this manuscript published in 1959, says that its date 'cannot be earlier than 734' but 'is not likely to be later than 737'.

The first eight lines of the page shown contain the end of Book III. There follow two lines showing that this is the conclusion of the book and the opening of Book IV. The remainder of the page contains a summary of the chapters of Book IV from 1-14. The following is a translation:

* No doubt Armorica is intended.

. . . [Bishop Jarman] doing many things with great wisdom as the priest, who was his companion on his journey and fellow worker in his teaching, told me; for he was a religious and good man, who travelled far and wide; and he led the people and the above-mentioned king back to the path of justice; and he did this so successfully that they deserted or destroyed the temples and altars which they had built, opened the churches, and rejoiced to confess the name of Christ Whom they had denied, desiring rather to die in Him with faith in resurrection than to live among their idols in the squalor of faithlessness. So when these things had been done, those same priests and teachers returned to their home rejoicing.

Here ends one book of 'The Ecclesiastical History of the English People'; here begins Book IIII of the 'Ecclesiastical History of the English People', with the chapter headings. I How, when Deusdedit was dead, Uighard (so that he might be consecrated to succeed him) was sent to Rome; but how when he himself died there, Theodore was ordained Archbishop and with Hadrian the Abbot, was sent to Britain. II How through Theodore all the churches throughout the lands of the English began to be taught the catholic faith and how Putta became Bishop of the Church of Rochester in place of Damian. III How Ceadd [Chad] of whom we have spoken above, was given as Bishop to the Kingdom of Mercia and concerning his life, death and burial. IIII How Bishop Colman, having left Britain, built two monasteries in Scotia, one for the Scots and the other for the English whom he had taken with him. V Concerning the death of Osuin and Ecgberct, and concerning the synod held at the place called Hertford, over which Archbishop Theodore presided. VI How Uynfrid was displaced, how Saexuulf received his bishopric and how Earconuald was given as a bishop to the East Saxons. VII How in the monastery of Barking a heavenly light was seen, showing the place in which the bodies of the virgin sisters were to be buried. VIII How, in the same monastery, a little boy who was dying called out that one of the sisters would follow him; and how she, when her soul was about to leave her body, caught a glimpse of the light she was to see. IX What were the heavenly signs that were shown, when the Mother of the community passed from the world. X How in the cemetery of that same monastery a blind woman, when praying, saw again and perceived the light. XI How King Sebbi, of that same kingdom, ended his life in the monastery. XII How Haeddi received the bishopric of the East Saxons in place of Letherius; Cuichelm, the bishopric of Rochester in place of Putta, and Gefmund in place of Cuichelm; and who were then the bishops in Northumbria. XIII How Bishop Uilfrid converted the province of the South Saxons to Christ. XIV* How on the Isle of Wight the Christians . . .

Page 136 Page from a late thirteenth-century manuscript (British Museum reference Egerton 3142) of the *Historia Britonum,* the *History of the Kings of Britain* by Geoffrey of Monmouth. The manuscript, in Latin, was compiled mainly at the Benedictine Monastery of St Benet at Hulme in Norfolk. The left-hand column shows the last chapters of Book I. The first of these gives the apocryphal story of the founding of London by King Lud. The opening chapter of Book II (right-hand column) tells of a Prince named Kamber, after whom the Welsh are called Cambrians to this day. These fantasies are typical of Geoffrey's work. The following is a translation:

But afterwards when Lud, the brother of Cassibellaun, who made war against Julius Caesar, obtained the government of the kingdom, he surrounded it with stately walls, and towers of admirable workmanship, and ordered it to be called after his name, Kaer-Lud, that is, the City of Lud. But this very thing became afterwards the occasion of a great quarrel between him and his brother Nennius, who took offence at his abolishing the name of Troy in this country. Of this quarrel Gildas the historian has given a full account; for which reason I pass it over, for fear of debasing by my account of it, what so great a writer has so eloquently related.

[Chap. XVIII.—*New Troy being built, and laws made for the government of it, it is given to the citizens that were to inhabit it.*]

After Brutus had finished the building of the city, he made

* Although XIV in this manuscript deals with the Isle of Wight this is Chapter XVI in most versions.

choice of the citizens that were to inhabit it, and prescribed them laws for their peaceable government. At this time Eli the priest governed in Judea, and the ark of the covenant was taken by the Philistines. At the same time, also, the sons of Hector, after the expulsion of the posterity of Antenor, reigned in Troy; as in Italy did Sylvius Aeneas, the son of Aeneas, the uncle of Brutus, and the third king of the Latins.

[BOOK II]

[CHAP. I.—*After the death of Brutus, his three sons succeed him in the kingdom*]

DURING these transactions, Brutus had by his wife Ignoge three famous sons, whose names were Loerin, Albanact, and Kamber. These, after their father's death, which happened in the twenty-fourth year after his arrival, buried him in the city which he had built, and then having divided the kingdom of Britain among them, retired each to his government. Locrin, the eldest, possessed the middle part of the island, called afterwards from his name, Loegria. Kamber had that part which lies beyond the river Severn, now called Wales, but which was for a long time named Kambria; and hence that people still call themselves in their British tongue Kambri. Albanact, the younger brother, possessed the country he called Albania, now Scotland. After they had a long time reigned in peace together, Humber, king of the Huns, arrived in Albania, and having killed Albanact in battle, forced his people to fly to Locrin for protection.

[CHAP. II.—*Locrin, having routed Humber, falls in love with Estrildis.*]

LOCRIN, at hearing this news, joined his brother Kamber . . .

INDEX

INDEX

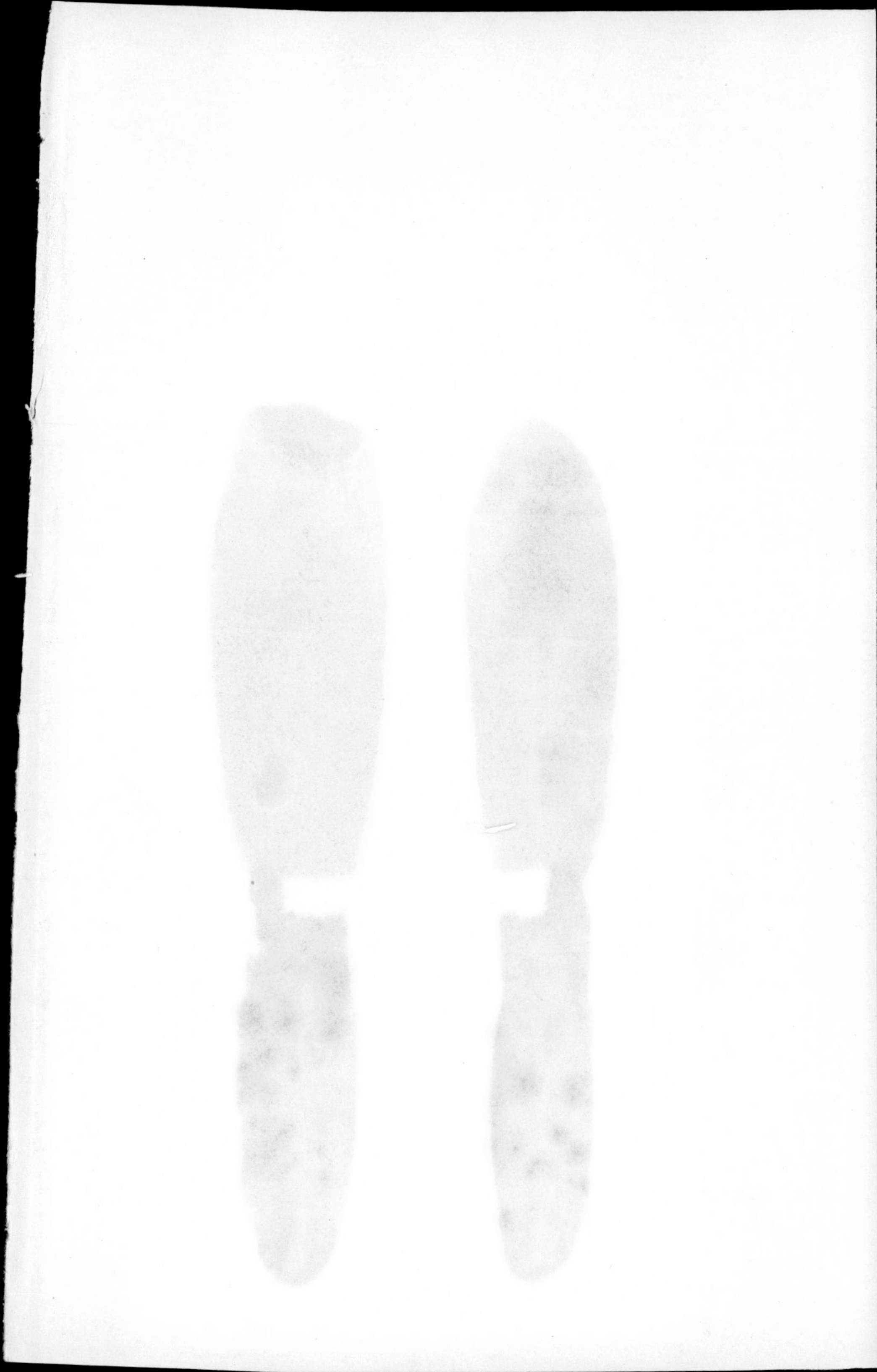